D0615105

A
GUIDE
FOR
SINGLE
PARENTS

A GUIDE FOR SINGLE PARENTS

TRANSACTIONAL ANALYSIS FOR PEOPLE IN CRISIS

By Kathryn Hallett

Celestial Arts
Millbrae, Ca 94030

To Hillary

First Printing, March 1974
Second Printing, January 1975
Library of Congress Card No.: 73-92524
ISBN 0-912310-55-3 Soft Cover
ISBN 0-912310-64-2 Hard Cover
Made in the United States of America

Library of Congress Cataloging in Publication Data

Hallett, Kathryn, 1937 —
  People in crisis.

  Bibliography: p.
  1. Transactional analysis. 2. Single-parent
family. I. Title.
RC489.T7H34   616.8'915   73-92524
ISBN 0-912310-64-2 Cloth Cover
ISBN 0-912310-55-3 Paper Cover

CONTENTS

FOREWORD

One of the most important aspects of autonomy and growth is a parent's ability to say goodbye after removal of the other parent through divorce, separation, desertion, or death. So many of us, when we have an opportunity in the here and now to be happy, either play games or fantasize in order to maintain our bad feelings indefinitely. I once lectured at a *Parents Without Partners* (PWP) meeting, stressing the games married partners play and how people continue those games with their ex-spouse after divorce.

"But Doctor," (one woman said), "isn't it awful when a husband does . . .?"

I answered her question and then said. "How long have you been divorced?"

"Twelve years." (Here she was still attending PWP, still angry with her ex-husband, as if sufficient anger would magically change the situation.)

Kathy Hallett writes extremely lucidly about saying goodbye. I would like to stress that newly single people often need to say goodbye not just to an ex-spouse, but to an entire past. I see a divorce not as an end, but as a beginning.

Robert L. Goulding, M.D., *Director*
Western Institute for Group & Family Therapy
Watsonville, California

Chapter 1

LETTING GO

Divorce, separation, desertion, or death are events that require "letting go" skills, especially when children are involved. From the time we're born we are taught how to say "hello," but seldom if ever do we learn how to say "goodbye." I clearly remember the day of my divorce and my anger that this "letting go" process had none of the elements of my marriage ceremony. No one was there to celebrate the end of a destructive relationship, or to advise me on my new state of single parenthood. There was little sign of community interest and no approval like the day of my marriage. There was no ritual to allow me, my children, and my husband to let go gracefully. I remember thinking that had one of us died, we would have at least received support in our grief.

As a child growing up in a large Italian family, I was taught the skills of mourning. I'll never forget the beauty and nobility of my grandfather's funeral. People mourned openly and loudly. It was no disgrace for a man to cry. Our family ate, slept, and participated fully in the farewell ritual. I watched as each member of the family kissed my grandfather goodbye. Even I, the smallest, shared in this. The scene may seem barbaric to some, but I felt everyone's love and imagined that grandpa was happy having so many people say goodbye to him. I had a similar feeling when witnessing the funeral of John F. Kennedy. I remember thinking how sensitive Jacqueline

Kennedy must be to permit the country to have this "letting go" experience. I admired her ability to create a ritual in which everyone could join.

Years later, when I watched Virginia Satir, a distinguished family counsellor, perform a divorce ritual, my children and I cried our tears and relived our own situation. I envied that couple and their children, for they had a chance to participate in the letting go process. I watched the woman remove her ring and give back the obligations that he had given to her. I listened to her tell what she would remember that was good and what she would forgive and forget. I looked at the children's faces as they watched their parents return their rings and promise to respect each other and continue to care, support and love their children. The couple cried, their children cried, and we all mourned the passing of an important event in their lives. We were there, too, when they rejoiced over their new freedom. The man told me they'd been divorced for two years and were continually "tearing each other up" until this day. They had refused to let go! Now he had shared his pain and joy with his entire family and could move on into a new relationship.

Most of us are not prepared for the crisis of death, separation, or divorce; nor do we have the opportunity to participate in such beautiful rituals. Generally, a person who has been through such an experience feels abandoned, torn, or split apart. We recognize our ambivalent feelings but simply don't know how to deal with them.

Part of this problem lies within our culture. We seldom learn the art of letting go. Any nurse will tell you how frustrating it is to deal with terminal patients and their families. Most of us, including the doctors, handle this stressful situation by avoiding it. Few of us acknowledge that death is inevitable or even painful. Until the end we cope unrealistically by repeating platitudes that we rarely accept any longer. A client of mine who was a terminal cancer patient was told, for example, "We will take care of you. Don't worry!" This isn't particularly reassuring when, in fact, she was experiencing enormous pain and had exhausted all possible medical routes. Her husband, on the other hand, felt anger and depression as he searched for ways to cope effectively with his impending loss.

The more we deny reality or ignore our feelings, the more disorganized and confused we become. Yet most people really do not know *how* to face such a crisis. What is needed is support, and even more important, people whose support and intervention allows the family to create their own resolutions based on reality.

We all read the term "mobile society" and know what that means. Yet at the time of crisis we *feel* what that means. Unfortunately, intervention by a concerned person is not as available in a mobile society. My generation found many sources of support for a family in crisis. The community was full of parents. Our neighbors were as involved in our lives as our aunts and uncles. Even the couple who ran the corner grocery store offered support. No one ever moved, or so it seemed, and the priest and minister called regularly. When a family was in trouble or a person died, the community was invested. Consequently letting go did not feel as lonely. There was always someone to nourish and nurture the grieving family or individual. In this atmosphere letting go was a normal process: painful but still healthy. At the time of saying "goodbye," there were many others to whom one could say "hello."

How to replace the extended family, or how to replace the lack of community concern, has become a problem of the times. Most people rely more and more on themselves and their own small unit or family. While we know that this limits our source of support, we have not yet found a substitute for our lost supporters. How do we stay integrated in an alienated society? Many people are turning more towards self help, or they pay to belong to a therapeutic group. Many of us trust that through reading we can help to understand ourselves better, and often we do.

This book is designed to help you learn the skills of letting go. It is my gift to you and your children who, like mine, may have experienced the same complex problems, feelings, and loss of integration at a time of change or crisis. In our family a divorce was the focal point of our problem. In yours it may be that, too, or any one of a myriad of events which require that you and the people you love adjust abruptly to new circumstances. In each case it will become possible to let go gracefully because of an astonishing breakthrough achieved in recent years in the field of psychology. This breakthrough is called Transactional Analysis (TA).

TA was developed in 1954 by the late Dr. Eric Berne, a psychoanalyst. His hope was to make the profoundly abstract ideas of his field comprehensible to the millions who were drawn to its precepts but who found it difficult to understand. In 1957 he published *A Layman's Guide to Psychiatry and Psychoanalysis,* and over the next decade this bold and creative thinker produced four more books of interpretation. While a relatively small following was developing for Dr. Berne's interpretations, he wrote a book that became a monument of its kind: *Games People Play.* Unable to find a publisher for it at first, Dr. Berne and a number of his friends sponsored and distributed the book. *Games People Play,* advertised almost solely through word of mouth, became one of the great best sellers in modern publishing history. It has been translated into at least fourteen languages; more than two million copies have been sold. It is used in seminars, lectures, and clinics throughout the world.

TA can help you, as it has helped tens of thousands of people in the short years since it was introduced. The "game" concept set forth in *Games People Play* has been applied successfully in the treatment of countless problems, including such diverse ones as juvenile delinquency, obesity, education, drug addiction, and alcoholism. Certainly it can be applied to the problem of letting go.

TA makes clear the Freudian concept that the human mind is comprised of a check and balance system—much like the Presidency, Congress, and Supreme Court. Freud called the principal elements of the personality the Superego, Ego and Id. Laymen often refer to the Superego as the Conscience, the Ego as the Self, and the Id as Desire. For Berne there was a clearer way to describe these parts. He realized that each person had three sources of feeling and behavior within him. They were not abstract concepts, however, but knowable, understandable, and recognizable realities. By knowing these parts, each person could sort out his own thoughts, feelings and behavior. He called these parts Parent, Adult, and Child.

When they are capitalized in this book, Parent, Adult, and Child will refer to ego states. When they are not, they will refer to actual parents, adults or children.

Unlike Freud's emphasis, which was sexual, the focus in TA is on the Child and his or her own sense of lack of self worth. Much of this sense of self worth comes from the Parent tapes which give most of us our understanding of what is "right" and "wrong." It is the Adult who deals with reality, calculates probabilities and is aware of alternatives. And, it is the Child who expresses feeling and who is creative yet rarely able to compromise when a crisis arises. As we grow we experience the life of our Child, Parent, and Adult. We all have memories which guide our behavior or trigger off our feelings. Eric Berne called these memories "tapes" because they resemble the data that can be stored by a tape recorder. He pictured them this way:

DIAGRAM 1

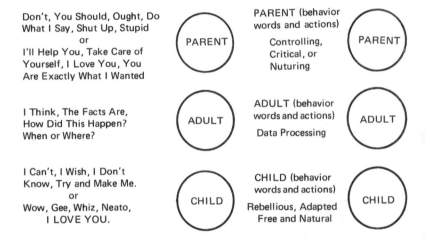

SIMPLE EGO STATES   DEFINED EGO STATES

Don't, You Should, Ought, Do What I Say, Shut Up, Stupid
or
I'll Help You, Take Care of Yourself, I Love You, You Are Exactly What I Wanted

PARENT

PARENT (behavior words and actions)

Controlling, Critical, or Nuturing

PARENT

I Think, The Facts Are, How Did This Happen? When or Where?

ADULT

ADULT (behavior words and actions)

Data Processing

ADULT

I Can't, I Wish, I Don't Know, Try and Make Me.
or
Wow, Gee, Whiz, Neato, I LOVE YOU.

CHILD

CHILD (behavior words and actions)

Rebellious, Adapted Free and Natural

CHILD

The Parent tape in your mind contains the advice, criticism, moral values, prejudices, and nurturing that your own parents gave to you. This tape is particularly crucial in times of stress because it tells you how you *should* or *ought* to run your life. Recorded here are all of the value judgments, moral decisions, and religious beliefs from parents, grandparents, older siblings, and other influential persons in your life. Depending on your collection of tapes, the recordings in your time of crisis can be critical, judgmental, blaming, or destructive. Or they can be nurturing, helpful, encouraging, and integrative. Here are just a few samples of destructive tapes that I've heard from people who sought counsel from me in the letting go process:

"I told you so. You should have listened to me!"
"You never did have any sense."
"What, therefore, God hath joined together, let no man put asunder."
"You're sinful and wrong."
"You made your bed, now lie in it."
"Carry your cross and bear your burdens. Don't change."
"I always knew he was a no-good bum."
"I always knew she would ruin you."
"Think of the children. They'll end up delinquents."
"You must have done something terrible to deserve this. God is repaying you."
"You've failed. You're unlovable. You're selfish and irresponsible."
"You'll be sorry when you're alone."
"You'll never make it alone."
"You're crazy to leave. You can't take care of yourself."

Frequently a person is unaware of the mental abuse going on in his or her head. Once we stop the critical tapes, however, most of us find there are an abundance of nurturing ones. If you listen closely, you'll hear other recordings.

"If you won't enjoy your differentness, it's better to part than continue harming each other."
"You have made the right decision." "I'll help you all I can."
"Your children will be okay." "You're a good person."

"Anyone can change their mind." "Anyone can make a mistake."

"It's okay to grieve over the loss of a loved one, but then you have to go on and love again."

A course in Transactional Analysis taught me to turn up the volume and frequency of my nurturing tapes and to turn off my critical ones. I learned to identify my Adult tapes, and through the help of other group members, added more information to strengthen the computer part of me. I learned my Adult ego state is the objective part of me which makes comments on my present situation. At a time of crisis, even these tapes become contaminated.

The diagram on the opposite page shows the three states of human personality.

The mind resembles a computer; and like a computer, it can be affected by contaminated data. Your Adult, for example, computes *all* the facts that you feed into it—even the wrong answers, if the wrong data are given to it. Suppose, for example, that you are a woman whose Adult says to you, "I'll need to get a job so that I can support myself after the divorce," and your Scared Child screams into the computer, "I haven't worked in so long, I'm no good for anything." This contamination is called a "delusion"—obviously everybody is good for *something*. But all too often it has its effect—the Adult, clinging to her Child, becomes emotionally crippled; her motivation is diminished and her actions limited.

Or suppose that you are a recently divorced man whose Adult tape says, "I will continue to see my children even though my wife has custody of them," and your Critical Parent tape replies, "Someone else will replace you." This contaminated Parent tape is called a "prejudice." Your former wife may remarry, but you don't have to be replaced as a father.

Or your Intelligent Adult says, "Statistics show that children of divorce are no more maladjusted than other children," and then on comes your Critical Parent with the remark, "Your children's grades are falling off since the separation; your son has become hard to manage."

In all of these internal dialogues, the interactions may be intense or even paralyzing to your body. Since the power of one tape is usually greater than the other two, you will act in the direction of its tendencies. How, then, can the most constructive tape be given sufficient power to give the personality a healthy direction? That is the goal and function of Transactional Analysis.

DIAGRAM 2

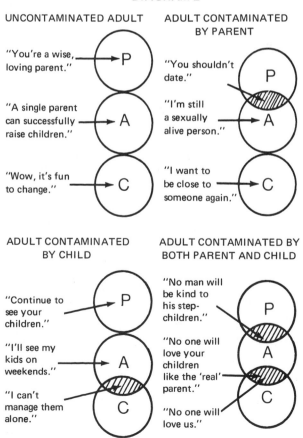

UNCONTAMINATED ADULT

"You're a wise, loving parent." → P

"A single parent can successfully raise children." → A

"Wow, it's fun to change." → C

ADULT CONTAMINATED BY PARENT

"You shouldn't date." P

"I'm still a sexually alive person." → A

"I want to be close to someone again." → C

ADULT CONTAMINATED BY CHILD

"Continue to see your children." → P

"I'll see my kids on weekends." → A

"I can't manage them alone." C

ADULT CONTAMINATED BY BOTH PARENT AND CHILD

"No man will be kind to his stepchildren." P

"No one will love your children like the 'real' parent." → A

"No one will love us." C

Chapter 2

TRAGEDY AND FULFILLMENT

Early in life, everyone writes his own story, or script. Gathering data based on the expectations others have for us, we establish goals and begin to work toward them. Usually our effort is unconscious, but often it is deliberate; writers, scientists, and other highly committed professionals often are able to look back and determine the precise point when they decided to pursue their activity with all available energy. Similarly, many of us begin at an early age to strive for money, fame, or love. And it is an amazing, unconscious characteristic of millions of people to strive for mediocrity or failure.

This tragic side of humanity has many causes, but the central one is that failure is the fulfillment of a prophesy made for us. Because of the early self-image given to us as children we sense that to fail is to do the "right" thing. At a point in life where our Adult tape makes a strong statement that will enable us to gain a healthier, more mature position, our Child, or perhaps our Critical Parent tape will intervene with a contaminating statement of its own. The result is confusion, delusion or failure. In many cases the individual begins to suspect that he/she has a natural gift for error! We recall that our script called for something like this. Almost gratefully we accept failure, thinking that "we got what we deserved."

In every crucial situation, it is important that you strengthen your Adult ego state so that it is not overwhelmed by your Parent and Child ego states. Letting go is one such crucial decision. Every internal statement can be examined so that you can think clearly and logically about the problems involved in letting go. When your Child or Parent tapes tell you not to let go, are they reflecting your parent's prejudice or delusions, or are they proposing action that will result in a fuller life to all of the people affected by the loss? The answer to this question is the key to "rational" behavior.

Women today offer an excellent example of how people can be programmed to live out their scripts. Our culture persuades women to believe they are unable to support themselves. They are raised to think their role is caring for others, and to be "second best" and to "stand behind" their powerful, assertive men! Consequently, they develop a wonderfully effective Nurturing Parent but neglect or ignore the fact that they also have an Adult which can be used outside the home. If they have used their Adult and worked before marriage, many of them assume that their computers are no longer useful in the outside world. The truth is, while the computer may have obsolete data, it can be restored to full effectiveness by putting new information into it. That takes work and energy—but it's worth it, to gain a new life.

Men, on the other hand, are persuaded by their scripts to use their muscles, to compete, and to think of themselves as fearless. The normal and healthy feeling of fear troubles some men when they discover it in themselves. They think they are being "cowardly," "unmasculine," or "womanish" when their hackles are raised, as they should be, by danger. Like women, men can also change these cultural or family notions. For fuller, richer lives we have to learn to feel our sadness and to express our fears. We have to understand that there is no such thing as an "all male" person or an "all female" one either. All of us are *people,* and we can learn to think of ourselves as human instead of male or female.

As we use and increase our ability to function well in *all* ego states, we decrease our feelings of impotency and helplessness. We are acknowledging and accepting all of our parts. While each part of you is important to your survival, one part, perhaps, is more significant than the others. It is your Child. Each of us knows a great deal about children and their need for love, care, and concern. What you've probably forgotten, however, is that *you* still have a Child within you. Watch your own children and you'll see how little difference there is between their feelings and your own when both are under pressure.

Your inner Child suffers most when you are under stress. This is a time when *you,* as an adult, need someone to hold, love, reassure, listen, and comfort you. It is often a time, however, when there is no supportive person in your life. Look at Diagram 2, page 15. Decide whether the family in your Parent-Adult-Child is similar. Ask yourself what you want to change in your life. If there is something, determine whether the Parent, Adult, and Child within you will permit you to do so.

The permission granted to you by your inner parts takes the form of an agreement, or contract. When your Adult wants to act and your Child tells you, "No, not now; first I need to be fondled," there is no inner certainty, agreement, or contract that will enable you to proceed. As a single person it's essential that you consult all of your parts before you permit yourself to move ahead. The alternative is to risk greater confusion and possible failure.

For example, Angie, a 32-year-old divorcee, wanted to express anger which she'd kept to herself during her marriage. Her contract to express anger would eliminate her need to store up these feelings and have one big rage once a year. Her Parent tapes, however, said "I won't love you if you're angry." Her Adult said, "It's OK for me to express angry feelings." Her Child said, "I'm afraid to be angry." It was easy for Angie to see that her Child feared some archaic Parent tape which threatened her with loss of love. When Angie realized she was no longer a little girl and didn't need her Parent's approval to survive, she had the ability to express anger without fear. Her contract was now a *redecision* since she no longer needed to hold onto a decision made long ago as a little girl.

Bill wanted a contract to get close to people after his divorce. He felt lonely and depressed in his apartment, yet feared reaching out to others. His Parent was saying, "If you get close, you'll get hurt." His Adult said, "If I am close to people, I won't be lonely and unloved." His Child said, "I'm afraid to get close and get hurt." Once Bill worked through his old decision (based on his father's desertion), he was able to see that his decision not to get close again was no longer useful. He may have needed the distance *then* to survive his hurt feelings, but he was only continuing *to hurt himself now* by avoiding others. Letting go of his hurt allowed Bill to reach out for people who would respond and relate to him intimately.

As a single parent, you are probably aware that your children also need and demand additional support and comfort in times of crisis. Both of you are undergoing the pain of loss and the grief of parting. Some of you may be experiencing the anger of your situation, or the bitterness of unequal responsibility, economic stress and unwelcome change. If you've been married a long time, you're probably used to that "someone" being there, even if the other person was not totally dependable or reassuring. If you were used to planning ahead with your spouse for the future, his or her departure or death may cause you to feel that your hopes and plans have also died. And even more important, if you anticipated feeling relieved and happy after the divorce, you may be wondering why you are emotionally drained or depressed. Whatever your unique circumstances may be, your Child is feeling less than whole. The Child within you may be crying, complaining, lonely, sick, angry, troubled, vindictive, guilty, resentful, impotent, confused or withdrawn. In extreme cases the Child within you may be temporarily deadened, shut off, or consciously controlled so that you feel nothing but emptiness. There are times when the human body shuts off all feeling in order to preserve the organism. This may be such a time for you. If you have turned off all your feelings, however, consider that this includes your good ones, too. You may want to learn how to "turn on" your Child again.

How can you help yourself and your children to acknowledge negative and conflicting feelings without shutting off? Can you maintain your good feelings even in times of crisis? TA has helped me answer these important questions. Membership in a TA group gave me permission, potency, and protection to take a look at myself and all my parts. Thus, I am able to discard the script that has handicapped me from the outset of my life. Through the careful inspection of my inner parts, I am able to know what *I really need and want.* I am able to fulfill myself. *In essence, I am now able to be me.* A startling example of a woman who had severe messages not to be herself is Ginny, who came into therapy after a short-lived, unsuccessful marriage. Ginny was twenty-four years old at the time, but none of her birthdays was a celebration of her.

Ginny had felt from the time she was six that she was supposed to be a boy. Her parents had never recovered from the loss caused by their son's death, who was two years older than Ginny. They had, in many subtle ways, encouraged Ginny to be the son who died, and stroked her for her boyish clothes, activities and apparent unwillingness to get along with girls. Ginny came into therapy saying "I don't know who I am." In the second session, Ginny found herself saying "I can't be me, I have to be Richard." Ginny's fear of losing her parents' love was so strong that we invited them into therapy. Within the group, her parents buried Richard and said goodbye, giving Ginny the permission to be herself. Ginny remained in therapy for six months as she worked out her resentment for her lost years, feelings and experiences due to her "Don't be you" injunction. Many of you may want to check out if you are living your life according to your expectations, or fulfilling the prophecy of your parent's predictions!

Chapter 3

WRITE A WINNING SCRIPT

Listen to your children relate their future hopes and expectations, and you'll see that very early we decide *how* we want to live our lives. My ten-year-old told her girlfriend she was going to be a veterinarian, marry a man who loved animals, and only have one child. This for her is a winning script. A thirteen-year-old I counseled recently stated: "I'm never going to get married. I hate men. I don't know what I'm going to do with my life. I'm too dumb to go to college. Sometimes I don't think I'll live very long because I'm always getting into trouble." This is a losing script. A young boy of sixteen said, "I never want to get married. Women are trouble. In fact, I don't like people in general. I'm going to spend my time in a lab where nobody bothers me!" Already this young man is predicting an isolated future. This is a "Leave Me Alone Script."

Take time *now* to write down what your script has been up until today. What did you decide you wanted from life? What goals did you have? Have you succeeded in reaching them? How do you feel about marriage? About being a parent? How do you feel about being a man or a woman? What are your feelings about sex? You can update your information on any of these topics by reading and evaluating where you are *now* in your thoughts and feelings. If you could rewrite your script, and have it any way you wanted, what would you choose to do with the next forty years?

Be honest with yourself. If you've never really wanted to be a parent, admit it. If marriage was not one of your goals, but a way of getting out of a sticky home situation, or reaction to social pressure, or even a means of economic support, admit it. If working is not what you want, or if the kind of work you do is boring and sheer drudgery, say so. No one is going to publish your findings! Take an honest look at what *you* really want for yourself *now*.

If you're finding it difficult to state what you want, listen to the recordings in your head again and discover how these tapes block the flow of healthy messages. Look at Diagram 3 and write out your own Flow Chart. When you cut out the flow of negative messages (Critical Parent) and put aside your feelings (Child), you'll find your Adult collecting only data on the problem. When all

DIAGRAM 3

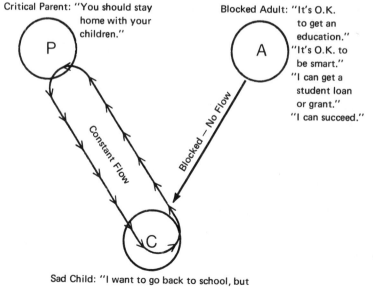

Critical Parent: "You should stay home with your children."

Blocked Adult: "It's O.K. to get an education." "It's O.K. to be smart." "I can get a student loan or grant." "I can succeed."

Constant Flow

Blocked — No Flow

Sad Child: "I want to go back to school, but I'll listen to you and feel sad."

the facts you want are put together, you can choose without interference or blocking. Remember, what you choose today can always be reevaluated. Take a risk and do things differently. Think of yourself starting at zero. If I take a risk—ask a man to dinner, apply for a new job, call a woman for a date, and I'm refused—I am still at zero. I haven't lost anything. I have, however, exercised my power to take risks and discovered that I will survive. I can be wrong, refused, or make mistakes. I am human. If my Adult agrees on the risk I want to take there is no way I can lose or go below zero.

I am aware that the word *no,* carries with it an emotional rubber band—that is, you swing back to the time when you were a small helpless child and were told "No." You are not a helpless child now, so if you're told "No," you can go elsewhere.

The diagram opposite this page illustrates how Adult input is blocked by the Child continuing to listen to Critical Parent messages. Your decision to act the way your parents wanted, or never to act a certain way again, is an outdated and archaic decision. In order to write your new script, you'll have to separate these messages so that the Adult information and data which you DO have, is allowed to filter through.

An example of a blocked trilogue is Addie, a forty-nine-year-old female, who came into therapy as a result of her daughter's delinquency. Addie had two teenage girls who had dropped out of school. One daughter was pregnant and the other was already supporting a child out of wedlock. Addie could see that the messages she gave them, and those that were given her were identical. Addie was aware that although she had chosen other ways to fulfill her script, the messages were still the same. She decided to work on her own problems in the hope that as she changed, the girls would have permission to change too.

Addie's stepfather had always told her she was a "baby doll" but not smart. She was stroked by him from the time she was three for being cute and pretty, but never for using her brains. After her marriage to Jim, she continued to act stupid and ignore responsibility for being either a wife or mother. When things got rough at home, Addie would run away just as she had from her original family, and feel justified in thinking her husband "should take care of everything." Since Addie was never told to stay in school or be educated, she criticized the school system and encouraged her own daughters to feel that learning was "stupid." All they had to do was get married, or find someone to take care of them. Addie's stepfather had given her permission to be a mother, however, and though Addie "felt like a child," she had given birth to four children she felt unable to raise. The care and education of the children was largely left to the father or to themselves. Since Addie had married a man very much like her stepfather, he gave them permission to be "beautiful dolls" and encouraged their promiscuous behavior by saying "girls are only good for cooking, cleaning and having babies."

When Addie made a decision to use her Adult, she was able to find employment as a personnel director, a job she really loved. She became comfortable with taking care of herself and being responsible. She offered her girls a more realistic and healthy model of an adult female. Her husband also came to therapy so they could work on revising and updating their beliefs and values. The years of living in script had left them with serious problems. Eventually, the two older girls entered therapy in order to get out of a "get away from" and "get nowhere with" life script.

After you've written your new script, imagine living

this way for ten years. How do you feel? Imagine living this way for thirty years and see if you still feel content with your choices. A woman who didn't want custody of her children discovered in twenty years she still felt great about her decision. She saw herself as a loving, kind, supportive parent, but not the custodial one. Her decision, *for her,* was a healthy one. In examining her husband's script, they discovered *he* really wanted the large family and was content to raise the children. She decided after the divorce to resume her studies in medicine.

Remember that while people are alike in many ways, it's OK to be different. If you already know that you love privacy, have little need or desire for intimacy or closeness and like to do things "your way," perhaps marriage isn't for you. Many females prefer their profession to child-rearing and household chores. Some men who are "married" to their jobs find they really enjoy being single again. If your idea of happiness is a place of your own unencumbered by other sounds and voices, settle for what you really want instead of what you think you "ought" to want.

Many people discover after a "split" that they can take care of themselves. It is not unusual for a woman to find out that singleness is OK. Males, on the other hand, object more strenuously to the single state, particularly if they've been dependent on a female. Discover if your dependency truly requires a woman, or if your learning to cook, clean and maintain your own wardrobe satisfies your needs. If, after you're able to function independently, you still want marriage, perhaps you really do want a woman for closeness and intimacy—not only to fulfill the role of mother.

In the case of death be sure you have said goodbye to your departed partner before you write your new script.

Often a bereaved person holds onto memories, fantasies, guilt feelings and resentments longer than is healthy. If the death of your partner left you with a residual of guilt feelings, forgive yourself for any real or imagined hurts, stop blaming yourself or using your guilty feelings to avoid loving again. As strange as it may sound, often guilt is a cover for resentment! Many people really feel resentful that they are left to carry the responsibility and burden of the marriage.

Marienne, age thirty-three, was a widow with two daughters. Before entering therapy, she confused her resentful and angry feelings with guilt. Most of her life had been devoted to a husband who for the last two years had been dying of cancer. Marienne felt angry and resentful that he had died prematurely, leaving her with small children to raise. She was frightened at the responsibility since she had few skills or education to support herself—much less them. Her husband, Ralph had no insurance, and her fear of being destitute and living on aid brought her to take a look at herself and her myths about her helplessness.

Before Ralph became ill, Marienne had never taken responsibility outside the home. She had never driven a car, used a checkbook or made an important decision without consulting Ralph. Since his death, she had withdrawn and was using this as an excuse to stay sad, depressed and alone.

At a session one evening, Marienne described her feelings as "cold and dead." She felt she had mentally and emotionally "crawled into the grave with her husband." She had given up on her own life.

During that session she made up her mind to say goodbye to him, and get on with meeting people and enjoying new relationships. She contracted to learn to drive and get into real estate—a vocation she had long wanted to learn. She further decided to sell their home which reminded her of Ralph and a life that was no longer realistic. She and her two daughters moved into an apartment. As Marienne took each step towards her own fulfillment, she gave up feeling helpless and frustrated. This she accomplished in two months having been "in her grave" for two years!

If yours was an "Until" or "After" marriage wherein both of you had planned to have fun "after" the kids grew up, or put off your own hopes and dreams "until" you had enough money, you may be feeling like Marienne, shortchanged and resentful instead of guilty.

Resolve to live your life *here and now* and consider you've learned a lesson from the "Until or After" script. Don't make your life a "Never" script by continuing to live in the past and future—*live now.* Help your children accept death as a natural consequence of life and encourage them to accept what is irrevocable. Let them express their feelings of abandonment or anger. Many children I know still insist, "If he loved me, he wouldn't have died." "If she had really cared about us, she would have taken better care of herself." Help your child to feel OK about living and loving others instead of holding onto the painful feelings of the parent's death.

In writing your own script, forget about what others want for or from you. Put aside the expectations your parents had for your life plan and give yourself permission to *think and feel for yourself.* Take a look at the sample script in Diagram 4 and see if you have similar injunctions. These are some of the most frequent messages which I've heard from people in the process of change. No one I know has ever had all of these injunctions, however, each one could contribute to your limiting yourself in significant areas of your life. Be aware that you receive messages from both *parents* and

DIAGRAM 4

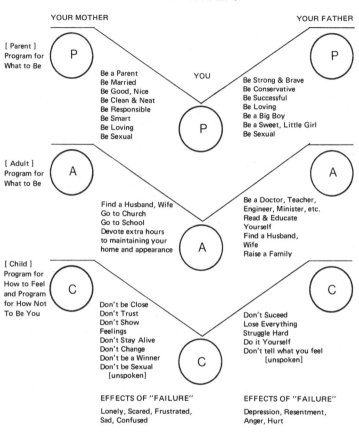

YOUR MOTHER   YOUR FATHER

[Parent]
Program for
What to Be

P

Be a Parent
Be Married   YOU
Be Good, Nice
Be Clean & Neat
Be Responsible
Be Smart
Be Loving
Be Sexual

P

Be Strong & Brave
Be Conservative
Be Successful
Be Loving
Be a Big Boy
Be a Sweet, Little Girl
Be Sexual

P

[Adult]
Program for
What to Be

A

Find a Husband, Wife
Go to Church
Go to School
Devote extra hours
to maintaining your
home and appearance

A

Be a Doctor, Teacher,
Engineer, Minister, etc.
Read & Educate
Yourself
Find a Husband,
Wife
Raise a Family

A

[Child]
Program for
How to Feel
and Program
for How Not
To Be You

C

Don't be Close
Don't Trust
Don't Show
Feelings
Don't Stay Alive
Don't Change
Don't be a Winner
Don't be Sexual
[unspoken]

C

Don't Suceed
Lose Everything
Struggle Hard
Do it Yourself
Don't tell what you feel
[unspoken]

C

EFFECTS OF "FAILURE"

Lonely, Scared, Frustrated,
Sad, Confused

EFFECTS OF "FAILURE"

Depression, Resentment,
Anger, Hurt

that often these messages are contradictory. One parent may want you to be an intelligent, professional female, and another parent may hope you marry and stay home with your children the rest of your life. Often a person experiencing conflict will identify the source when his/her script is presented. It's up to *you* to decide what you want now, and let go of past decisions.

Since scripts are written when we're small, they're generally not reliable guides for future adult planning. A decision made at age six to have eight kids (like mom did) can prove disastrous if your Adult wasn't in on the planning later on. Decisions on how to live, whom to love and how to love are generally made without proper adult information. As a child you probably made decisions out of fear. You decided that if you didn't do things "their way" you'd lose your parents' love and approval.

You may have decided to be the way other people expected you to be and put away many of your own dreams, thoughts and feelings. A child who is disappointed by his parents' divorce, or who has lost a parent through death, may well decide never to get close to another person again. A child whose feelings are ignored or shut off may decide never to tell or show how she/he feels again. A child who is overprotected or kept "the baby" may continue to seek people who care and protect him/her. Another child who is left by parents to handle his younger brothers and sisters long before he's able might feel he can only be loved if he takes care of others.

Parents who script their daughters for only being wives and mothers can produce females who fear using their brains outside their homes. These women feel uneasy about asserting themselves or showing "aggressive" feelings. After a divorce or the death of a partner, they may feel frightened at the notion of leaving home. They may feel inadequate financially to take care of themselves or to take over the disciplining of their children.

Men who have been scripted to work hard and succeed may find it difficult to relax, enjoy and let their *Child* out. They may see marriage and childrearing as "duties" and not creative opportunities for growth. A child who was told he would wind up like his "drunken" father, or go broke and lose everything he had like "Uncle Henry" may do that very thing.

Many people I've counseled believe "It's in my genes," which is another way of saying, "I can't be helped or changed." Someone told them that this was the way it was going to be and they bought that lie. There is no need to continue buying into a losing program. If you find yourself saying, "I sure wish I were different, but something stops me," consider that which is stopping you is your script—*you.* You can change. You can get help and start now without stopping. First, however, you'll have to paint a clear picture of the chapters already written.

Diagram 4 shows how a losing script develops. You can insert your own messages and determine how these messages keep you stuck to a script written for you as a five-year-old. You may have been the co-author since you had to agree at one time to follow the instructions, but it's time you published your own script and take credit for your life.

Since the loss of a family can be one of the most tragic and lonely experiences a human can face during a lifetime, evaluate how your script contributed to this drama. If you found that you identified with the Victim role in the first chapter, or realize you played the role of drama. Find out who wrote your script and change it if you need to. If being a "rescuer" to an alcoholic, drug addict or gambler was your past, avoid these characters in the future. If physical or mental abuse occurred during your relationship, discover what messages you're giving yourself. You don't have to be beat on. If your spouse was engaged in any criminal activities, ask yourself how you relate to Losers.

For those of you who've come close to taking your own life, or had serious doubts about living, get professional help and learn how to give up your "Don't Exist Script." Until you've made a firm decision to live—no matter what happens—you won't collect good feelings. Until you have redecided the most crucial script question, you'll only perpetuate your bad feelings. In addition, you'll proceed to gather evidence and incidents to validate this lethal decision. Once you've collected enough depressed, angry or hurt feelings, you may act on this decision and eventually destroy yourself.

The word suicide is still taboo, since many people refuse to admit someone can become so desolate that they end their own life. Statistics show that the single parent is more inclined toward suicidal thoughts and actions, and also less likely to call for help. One person dies by his own hand each minute. One person dies every five minutes in an accident. Both can be avoided. More divorced men take their lives than divorced females, and, although this could be attributed to male aggressive scripting, the female usually has her children and isn't as isolated as the male single parent. Further, females are scripted to be more nurturing. During times of stress, a woman's library of tapes usually has more lifesaving messages than a man's. Bereavement, financial stress, joblessness, domestic difficulties, confusion, and withdrawal are all part of the single parent syndrome, and are contributing factors in the suicidal plan. Take yourself seriously and take those around you seriously. If you or anyone you know has made statements like the following, pay attention. Talking about dying is not only a bid for attention, but also a plea for help. No one, if given healthy options, would choose to destroy themselves.

"I can't go on."

"What's the use of living."

"I'd be better off dead than alive and worth more, too."

"I'd like to cash in my chips."

"I'd like to drive my car right off that cliff."

"I'd like to lie down and never wake up again."

"If I died, he/she would be sorry."

"Everyone would be better off without me."

"If I died tomorrow, those kids wouldn't even miss me."

These are suicidal statements. If you've heard someone talk this way, you can be sure that they are at least "playing" with the notion of suicide. This person needs professional help. If this person is you, *don't take your life*. Find out how to change those messages and remember that they weren't your idea to begin with. Discover that "I don't want to die; this is someone else's idea." Each of us came into the world with a will to live. We still have the will to live only we don't know how. Learn HOW to change your script to an EXIST script and don't exit before you're 110.

Remember, whatever you discover during your self-examination can help you redecide. It's OK to change. It's OK to live. You no longer need the love and support of your parents to survive. You're capable of taking care of yourself now. If you're temporarily unable to do so, get help until you can. Don't be embarrassed to admit you need protection during a crisis. Remember 80 per cent of the population has admitted to feelings of depression at one time or another. You aren't sick or crazy. You're a worthwhile human being who deserves help. You're listening to messages that are scaring you, and you can find out how to stop scaring yourself.

Remember, too, that if your parents gave you

destructive messages, it was not their intention to destroy you. Human beings, *all of us,* are capable of sending unhealthy messages out of our pain and unawareness. Learn to distinguish between good and bad messages or advice. Learn to listen to the tapes in your head and resolve to decide for yourself whether or not you'll continue following their advice. You can say. "No, I won't listen to that." Or you can say, "OK, that sounds like a good idea." You can "grow yourself" up again by choosing your own goals and by taking responsibility for your choices. Be a firm, strong Parent to yourself and let go of the past. Remember that a whole, integrative person has the ability to flow from one ego state to another. Don't allow yourself to stay locked in one position.

Cooperate with your Child in the growing up process. If you kill your Child, or ignore and neglect the Child in you, your Parent won't have anyone to talk to much less carry out instructions. Remember that an autonomous person has a creative Child who has Adult awareness and Parental approval. If your Child is rebellious and used to acting impulsively, look for the Critical Parent in your head and refuse to respond with rebellion. Shut off the controlling tapes and act spontaneously instead of impulsively.
goals and direction, particularly if your script was a tragic one.

Ward and Sue came into treatment when Ward made an attempt on his life. Both of them realized that they were in a tragic script of suicide, work and failure much of their married life. Ward's dad had been an alcoholic and ran out on his wife when Ward was fourteen. Ward had never seen him since, but still carried a mental picture of a man who was "helpless, hopeless and all kid." Sue came from a family where the women took care of the men since Sue's dad was frequently drunk.

Both of their backgrounds set them up for an unhappy marriage for themselves. Neither one had known happiness at home. Ward found all his excitement in the barroom, while Sue got her good feelings from the work she did. Home was a place to fight, struggle and feel rejected. Both had felt sure when they married they would not give their children the hard time they experienced. Each had fantasies of raising their children with plenty of love, material goods and companionship. In fact, however, their two children were experiencing much of what Sue and Ward had lived through in their early years.

Becky, age nine, said she was terrified her dad would kill one of them when drunk. Mark, who was twelve, vacillated between being helpless to protect his mother, and angry with his dad for not taking charge of himself. Both children were having problems in school, and appeared to be well on their way to falling victims of this marriage.

The parents made a contract to stay in group and work through the messages causing Ward to drink instead of think! Ward gave up alcohol altogether even though two months later his feelings and behavior had not altered much. For Ward there was much work and pain as he learned to use his capacity to think and deal with feelings and not escape or withdraw into his room.

Sue had to deal with her resentment for all the years she remained in an unhealthy environment. She was aware that being close to anyone was a threat and that Ward's drinking made it easy for her to work hard and avoid intimacy. She changed her job so she would be home the same hours as Ward and made a decision to trust him with responsibility for the first time in their marriage.

For Ward and Sue, trust was a large factor in their relationship since they had no reason, growing up in their families, to gain such feelings. They certainly had not felt them in their own relationship. They agreed to see each other as fresh and new and not dig around in the past to stay with old business and bad feelings.

This couple had such destructive injunctions that it was a sign of their tremendous desire to live and be well that caused them to change rapidly and effectively. They remained in group for one year—or a total of ninety-six hours. Ward has been off alcohol for two years and "counts his candles" from the day of his last drink.

Just as your children like to be patted and stroked for their good behavior, so does the Child in you want and enjoy strokes for change. How you go about getting reinforcement and positive strokes depends on your circumstances. Sue and Ward chose transactional analysis. If you're a member of a church, you may choose pastoral counseling, or gain strokes from members in your congregation. If you belong to an organization like PWP, you'll gain encouragement and strength from other members who are changing with you. Your children, like mine, will stroke you as you move out and enjoy yourself. They will respond to your winning behavior and feel they, too, have permission to be winners.

You may want to join a TA group of women or an all male group and discuss your script changes with a TA therapist. Or, you may feel the need of working with only one person on your script changes. Whatever your decision, it's important that you share your new life with others.

I've known numerous people who've found making contracts for change in a TA group helpful in clarifying their goals and in acting on them swiftly. Membership in this group assures supportive interest and concern for your healthy survival. A TA group doesn't deal with "approving" or "disapproving" behavior—simply behavior that is healthy and satisfying to you.

Until you decide what kind of outside support you need or want, remember it's OK to stroke yourself. You can give yourself strokes for being and for doing. I find that telling myself, "Hey, Wow, I did that. I'm terrific." is as important as having others tell me I'm OK.

Chapter 4

FEELING OK

At the time of my divorce I felt good about my decision. Before long, however, I received messages to the contrary. People consoled me, as if something terrible had happened. That conflicted with my concept that I had taken a healthy step. Furthermore, my own Critical Parent tapes were running at full speed. Some of the fears and prejudices that I had suppressed, in my eagerness to get the divorce, came to the surface.

I'm sure that many of you entered your single state with confidence and courage to change your lives and immediately faced obstacles and objections. It is nonsense to say that other people don't affect our lives; they do, powerfully. Indeed, transactions with other people not only are necessary for pleasure, but for sanity. How do we know which are helpful and which harmful? The ability to detect and deal with the harmful ones is the most important skill that a single parent can acquire.

Transactional Analysis has helped me gain this skill. The first step was to enter a group that was able to grant me permission. Having it, when I wanted to act, I was able to choose between the early script, given to me by my parents, and the one that I wanted to write for myself. I knew that if I decided to refuse my parents' advice the Child within me would feel scared, anxious, depressed, confused, or guilty. The members of the group offered me strength to resist these feelings and pressures. Through their reassurance and warm support they were saying to me, "If your 'kid' gets scared, call me," or "If you find yourself anxious and unable to listen to your nurturing tapes, come in; we'll talk." In this way the group offers permission to change by offering power and potency. Since children see their parents in this role they need, as adults, to feel their own potency and power so that they can permit themselves to change without fear of punishment or loss of love.

The first step for me was to identify the three people inside me—Parent, Adult, and Child, and become aware of my thoughts and feelings. When these three parts function well, I'm a whole, loving, joyous and creative person. The fact that one part is not together is no indication that I'm falling apart, sick, crazy or incompetent. When you and I recognize that we have LEARNED to run these tapes, we can then learn to run new ones.

You can also learn to be a kind Parent to yourself in the growing process. Remember how long it took your children to walk, talk, and read? Give yourself the same encouragement and understanding that you gave them. Stop grading yourself by the mistakes you make, and give yourself pats and promotions for recognizing self-defeating behavior. Look around and borrow tapes that are nurturing from other people. Understand and talk to the Child within you as you would your own child. Reassure your Child that you do care about her or his feelings. Hold your Child close to you and protect her when frightened, comfort him when sad and acknowledge your Child's angry feelings. Turn your Child's angry energy into constructive action by using your negative feelings to motivate healthy actions.

Ask yourself what your Child wants and then get it! Pamper your Child. For some of you, purchasing new clothes, a trip out of town, dinner out, long distance calls to loved ones or a new car is a way of saying to your Child, "I'll take care of you." For others, a new piece of furniture, books, records, flowers, or simply putting yourself FIRST are ways of telling and proving to your Child that you really care.

If you've been used to fulfilling other people's needs for so long that you've lost sight of your own, begin there. Take time to relax and give yourself permission to dream again. Recall all those past hopes and wants you may have put aside over the years. If you're a man maintaining two jobs now to support your family, and take no time or money for play, re-examine your situation carefully. If you exclude your Child, you will pay a dearer price in the end. Watch your own children and see what happens when they feel uncared for, neglected and unloved. If you find yourself cranky, tired, rebellious, physically sick or tense, chances are you have neglected your Child. When my own children show signs of stress, I am aware that they need more nurturing. After a divorce there is usually less Nurturing Parent around. Physically, one parent is no longer available to nurture every day. The other parent is typically drained, or struggling to maintain his/her own equilibrium. I know at times I felt there was no Nurturing Parent in the home at all.

Allow others to nurture you, too. Being taken care of by others is a way of restoring yourself and your own good feelings. Shortly, after my divorce I found much of my nurturing outside the home. People I worked and went to school with listened to my Child and took care of my needs. I used to think of myself as a cup which felt empty at times. When I reached out for others to fill my cup, I always received.

A divorced woman in a group of mine recently gave herself permission to take long, luxurious baths followed by a manicure, something she'd given up long ago. A father of four treated himself to a trip to Disneyland— something his Child had wanted for a long time. A mother of three with a limited budget arranged for a group member to care for her children for three days. This was her first vacation in fourteen years. Each of you wants something. Instead of waiting, get it now!

Take a look at the diagram showing contamination and make up your own diagrams. Allow yourself to talk aloud so you recognize the voices within you and identify which ego state is active. Which ego state solves your problems. Do you listen to your Critical Parent or your Child? What does your Adult say? Begin decontaminating your PAC tapes now. Do the same for your children when they have conflicting feelings and thoughts. Most of all, consider what my three-year-old told me at the time of my own personal despair, "You won't always feel this bad, Mommy!"

Why are so many recently divorced people "Not —OK"? The chief reason is that they are carrying on destructive transactions. One Transactional Analyst, Steve Karpman, devised a way to illustrate these transactions. He showed them in the form of a triangle which is shown below. This triangle demonstrates

DIAGRAM 5

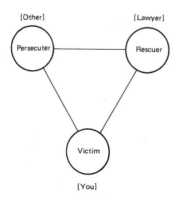

how the particular stance a person takes affects his feelings and behavior. As long as we are part of a triangle there is no way for us to be whole people. We are forever at one corner of the triangle or another. Thus, we can never link all of our parts.

The single parent is rarely whole. Usually she/he is in the Victim slot or in the role of Persecutor. Diagram 5 shows the triangle and various switches that each person can make. The theory of the triangle rests on a well-founded observation: once you choose a position in a human relationship, the odds are that you will move to another before the drama is over. When you choose, find a position outside the triangle that will enable you to be OK. Don't force yourself into a slot that eventually will destroy you. By carefully analyzing your position and giving yourself room to grow, you permit yourself to be a whole person. If in your previous relationship you played the role of Victim, you won't change your life significantly by shifting to the Persecutor's slot. To be truly healthy you must be autonomous, responsible, and whole. The only way to accomplish this is to leave the triangle and relate to people outside of it. Or, as Karpman suggests, decide to be heard and not hurt; mate instead of hate; and be smarter, not a martyr!

Chapter 5

BEING OK ECONOMICALLY

Typically, when applying for legal help, the single parent is cast in the role of Victim. Law is a profession of advocacy. Although in some states there are new rules permitting "no fault" divorces, in many others lawyers are expected to maintain that their clients have been wronged in some way. In this situation the other partner in the marriage usually is seen as the Persecutor. This places the lawyer in the powerful role of Rescuer, since it's his duty to protect and defend the rights of the "Victim." (See Diagram 5, page 41).

The children, in effect, also are relegated to the Victim slot. A young friend of mine, aged ten, once told me that when his parents divorced "I felt like a piece of furniture the way they split me up between them." Another little girl who was six at the time of the divorce said, "Nobody even asked *me* what I wanted. They decided without even asking me what I FELT." Children don't have to be Victims, but placed in a Victim slot, they *feel* victimized or helpless to take responsibility for their own life and direction. Consequently, the Victim will begin to Persecute the other party until that party feels like the Victim. In the end, however, if this was his/her chosen spot, he will return to that position when establishing his own family.

A classic example of this is Jack, age forty-two, who came into therapy after experiencing a divorce which left him depressed, without his children and the comfort of his own home. As a child, Jack knew what it was like to be a child in a single parent family. Many of the feelings he had now were similar to those he had experienced when his father left his mother. Jack was four at the time of the divorce, but he remembered feeling sad and alone. He also remembered that he decided he could not make it without his dad, and felt all his life he had never felt "whole or satisfied."

Jack put all his emotion aside at the age of five and determined to "be good and work hard." His mother would not have any more "burdens"! His step-father resented the care of Jack, which only increased his feelings of being a "burden" or unwanted member of the family. When Jack married, he was certain he and Phyllis would create a home that would make up for what he never had as a child. The first seven years of their marriage were good ones. He and Phyllis had three daughters and were able to buy and maintain comfortable surroundings. All went well until the birth of their first son, Phillip.

Jack never understood why Phyllis resented this child as she seemed loving of the girls. From the time Phillip was born, he felt she looked for signs of illness in the child. Eventually, she was able to substantiate that Phillip was retarded. Often she would say, "He's a burden on us" and Jack's old feelings returned. When Phillip was ten, he was committed to a home for retarded children though Jack felt this was unwarranted. He was sure his son was psychologically disturbed and really quite bright. From the time Phillip was removed from the home, the marriage was psychologically over.

Although he visited his son, and maintained a weekend visitation privilege with his daughters, Jack felt alone. He was depressed and considered killing himself several times. How Jack depressed himself was clear. He refused to show any anger toward his situation and remained in a passive, helpless position. He preferred feeling bad rather than risk acting to resolve his difficulties. Often in the group he would ask for suggestions about his son, and then refuse to take them. "Oh, that won't work," he'd say. When a group member told him that *he* was keeping himself and his son deprived of a home—he blew up. Many of his sad feelings disappeared as he screamed and shouted at the father who left him and the mother who put her husband before Jack. He buried his father once and for all, although his dad had long since been dead! Eventually, he bought a home and managed to get Phillip out of the institution. He would not perpetuate the same messages with his own child. Jack was not willing to work on his feelings about women, and remained detached and aloof even though he realized his life lacked much in the way of completeness.

I've seen children, who like Jack, persecuted their parents for their mistakes. I've observed women persecute their partners long after legal proceedings are over, and men refuse responsibility for the care, custody and financial support of their offspring. All of these people continue to victimize their families. I've observed lawyers who began as Rescuers, end up as the Victims or Persecutors. In the first case they are dismissed by one party as having been inadequate, i.e., failed to persecute hard enough. In the latter example, they turn persecutor when the parties refuse to pay for legal services and advice.

Since I have worked for family law lawyers, I'm convinced that the law office is seldom the place for humane negotiations. The very structure of the law, in most states, contributes to the triangle and oppresses people already sufficiently hassled. The entire legal game is designed in such a way as to establish blame, fault, guilt, and wrong doing. It's possible, however, for single parents to insist on humane, legal treatment. You and your lawyer can establish an understanding of how your proceedings will be conducted. Be clear with him about your desire not to persecute, and choose a lawyer as you would a family physician. He must have a Nurturing Parent in addition to a good Adult. My favorite family law lawyer, Jim Struif, tells me the range and scope of various state laws differ widely and change rapidly—only a lawyer can guide you gracefully through the labyrinth of details. When a divorce is contested, you especially need to consult a competent family law attorney.

If you're a woman, your lawyer must understand that you have probably spent the major part of your time and energy—not to mention your prime years—maintaining your children, husband and home. Since you weren't paid in salary for the job you did, your financial position or earning power is probably nil. While I don't advocate stripping your partner of his assets, I feel strongly that the woman and children must not be deprived of adequate financial support. Most support payment scales are drawn up by men who have not purchased clothes, food or other necessities for growing children and are hopelessly inadequate. A lawyer I know thought children's shoes still cost $4.00.

In addition, men are often unaware of the cost of child care since it was formerly free. Although a man may feel that his $100.00 a month is ample support for his child, he may not realize that *child care alone* may cost his wife $200.00 a month. Indeed, when I left our four children for one month, my husband was stunned to discover he spent over $600.00 to maintain the children. Part of this was child care, and part was services which I perform, such as laundry, cooking and cleaning. As a busy professional man he had never considered doing these jobs himself. He soon discovered that the cost of caring for children was indeed more than he anticipated. Most females, who work outside the home, however, still maintain most of their jobs. Still, child care, particularly when the children are young, can absorb most of the salary that the average single person can make. In addition, I know of few professions that pay women the same rates as men. Although this is changing because of the women's movement, females are still largely responsible for child care and earn less money to boot.

Since most men do not have custody of their children and have not participated actively in the child rearing process, they are unaware of the cost and demands of child rearing. When my lawyer asked me to make a list of "all my children's expenses," I almost laughed though I felt more like crying. Later, I did cry, when I discovered I was saying "No" to many legitimate requests simply because I did not have the money. I have known many women who feel guilty and upset when they have to tell their children "No, I can't pay for haircuts, new shoes, school pictures, movies or dog food;" both *children* suffer. When a man realizes he can't afford to take a woman out after his divorce, buy a stereo, or even make a long distance call, he is aware that divorce is not only emotionally expensive, but economically, too. When all parties feel they cannot afford dental work, or new glasses, and certainly no more vacations, the Child suffers, and the Nurturing Parent feels inadequate to support and care for that Child.

At this time, the Adult can step in and compute how two families will survive where possibly there was economic trouble as one. Ideally, the Adult of both will determine how to increase the family resources, and not permit any member of the family to suffer so that one person has freedom.

Remember, too, that the law punishes a mother by imprisonment for neglect of her children. The law does not punish society, however, for allowing mothers and children to live without sufficient funds. When I taught deprived children I was aware of many divorcees who were persecuted for leaving youngsters at home in the care of older children. Many mothers worked shifts and were unable to pay for outside help. The nursery, which was less expensive, did not open until 8:00 a.m. Consequently, an older child would sit until school opened. If a toddler was sick, an older child would stay home and care for that child. The school, community and law all persecuted an already persecuted parent. If, however, the mother stayed home and collected welfare checks, she was again persecuted for not earning her own living.

Since women are scripted to be "nice, cooperative and lady-like," they seldom think to use their aggressive powers to insist on fair and equitable treatment. Many will tell their lawyers, "I don't care what he pays me so long as I don't have to fight." I think fighting is necessary and useful, particularly when the Adult is directing the fight. When parents in a community fight for better day-care centers they are using their anger constructively. When they insist on free medical services or reduction in food prices, they are winners.

Explain to your lawyer that each of you, and this includes your children, are letting go in an effort to rebuild your lives. *You don't want to destroy each other, or be destroyed.* Negotiate so that each of you can survive with a minimum of stress. Most games played by single parents are a result of unfair negotiations, or an unwillingness to let go. I had no hostility toward my former husband because he offered to pay alimony until I completed my education. If, however, your partner was truly irresponsible before the divorce, persecution will not change that pattern. People seldom change through punishment.

Chapter 6

THE SOCIAL PROBLEMS

It is astonishing how many people and institutions reinforce the idea of the triangle in their relationships with single parents. Schools and churches often do so, even out of well-meaning efforts. They may be staffed by people who will make your children feel themselves to be Victims. To change this attitude will take a social upheaval; at best you can do whatever you can to counteract it.

I don't believe that we have to change others in order to survive. I do believe that we can and must change ourselves. We can choose better options and continue to maintain our own sense of values, even while we are living among values with which we don't agree.

If teachers refuse to hold children responsible for their behavior and instead say, "What can you expect of Paul, his mother is divorced," you can anticipate that Paul will cop out. If a school counselor says, "How can that poor child study when she's upset about her father," you don't have to agree. There is a time for understanding and sharing a child's loss and a time for getting on with living. As for the role the ministry plays in divorce, I am convinced that many attitudes and criticisms are non-verbal. For instance, I don't recall any specific words that indicated I was not welcome at church, however, I was aware of an uncomfortable feeling towards me after the divorce. I was aware also that discussion of family outings or couples activities were also avoided around me. I'm still not sure how a single female threatens married couples. Of course, some religions specifically denounce the divorced person and insist they have sinned. I see the church frequently acting in the role of a Critical Parent, and I'm aware that either a Child responds by saying "I will leave the church," or "I will stay and feel bad." A divorced female in one of my groups continues to attend church and feel guilty when everyone receives communion. Her Child feels like an "outcast." How much healthier and truly Christian would it be to accept a person and continue to love, support and nurture them at this time of stress.

Fortunately some attitudes have altered, and children living with one parent are not as unusual as they were ten years ago. It's not uncommon, for example, to find many children today who have no father to attend the Father's Day Banquet, nor is it strange to find children whose mothers work and can't attend school functions. Any community, school or church activity, however, which reminds your children of their loss will continue to set off "not OK" feelings, unless your children are prepared to deal with them.

Don't allow your children to use these occasions to feel victimized. I found that refusing to let my own cash in on bad feelings forced them to take responsibility for these times. Give your children sufficient information so that their Adults can handle the situations. Essentially they need to know that *the absence of one parent doesn't mean they are unloved or loved less.* Point out alternatives such as inviting a good friend, grandparent or uncle, or sharing a parent. Remind your children that the absent parent spends special times with them alone, and refuse to be blackmailed or responsible for their bad feelings. Once your children decide to be Victims, there will *always* be a reason to feel bad. Sometimes, just asking them, "Do you want to go and feel bad, or go and feel good?" confronts children with their responsibility and control for their own feelings.

Here is a typical conversation. You can change the names and events, the feelings are probably the same.

> *John:* "Dad, will you come over to scout meeting to-night? *All* the parents are coming."
>
> *Dad:* "No John, your mother and I decided we wouldn't attend meetings together, and it's your mother's turn."
>
> *John:* "*Everyone* else will have both parents. Why can't you come? I *know* you don't care or you'd come."
>
> *Dad:* (Since these conversations are usually on the phone, dad is at a disadvantage to *show* John he cares. He is further at a disadvantage since he can't see John's face. John's voice, however, indicates that he is going to cry.) "Look, John, I understand how you feel. I know you feel crummy that mom and I aren't there together like we used to be. I understand you feel different from the other guys."
>
> *John:* "*NO, YOU DON'T UNDERSTAND.* You *never* understand. You'd rather stay home with your new family. *You care more about them.*" (Now John *is* crying.)

At this point Dad is aware that John is in his Child. He realizes that Adult information will not be heard until John feels nurtured and cared about. His Child will not listen to *facts.* So Dad proceeds to reassure John.

> *Dad:* "Hey, I've got an idea. I'll pick you up after pack meeting and we men will go out and

celebrate your new merit badge. You can invite a friend if you want to, or we'll go alone to that ice cream place you like."

John: "I just want you *there.*" (Now, Dad hears that John is listening even though he has not given up the fantasy that life will always be like it was before the divorce.)

Dad: "I will." (And he is, too, if he wants to maintain his son's trust and respect!)

I remember holidays and birthdays were a bad time at our house shortly after my divorce. Both of the children wanted their father home "like it was before." The holiday brought excitement and also pain until I finally confronted my daughter and myself with the reality of our situation.

Regan: "Mom, why don't you invite Dad for Thanksgiving?"

Me: "I don't want to."

Regan: "But, Mom, it would be so nice to have him here. *You're selfish.*"

Me: "Regan, your father has his own family now."

Regan: "I bet they would all come. What's the matter with all of them coming?"

Me: "I know you would like to have your Dad here because you love him. I remember too, how much fun he was on Thanksgiving. I know what you're feeling. *I miss him too.*"

Regan: "Well, then, invite him!" (The Child's solution is so simple!)

Me: "I feel hurt watching him love another woman. I feel left out. I don't want to feel bad, Regan, and yet I don't like seeing him love someone else when I'm alone. Do you understand that?"

Regan: "Yes. I wouldn't like that either. *But, I still want him here.* I feel lonely when he's not here! You remember how he always sang those goofy songs? And remember when he broke that wishbone with me? *Please, Mom, do it for me.*"

Me: "You can spend Thanksgiving Day at their house, Regan. I don't mind your doing that, or you can stay here with us. I won't invite them to our home. I think we all believe that someday we'll be together again. We are not ever going to be a family in *that* way again." (There was a long pause here as both of us absorbed that reality clearly and openly.)

Regan: "If Dad would leave that woman, and if you would take him back, then we could." (Now, she is crying and I am sure that she has had that fantasy all along. I am aware that most children have the fantasy that some day, somehow they will get their parents together again.)

Me: I share her tears, and hold her. Afterwards, I am able to say again to her, "Regan, your father and I will *never* live together again. Where do you want to spend the holiday?"

Regan: "I'll go to Dad's. You're sure you won't mind?"

Me: "Nope, I'll save the wishbone for you!"

Chapter 7

COLLECTING GOOD FEELINGS

A human being will shrivel up and die without contact. If your contact is minimal or unrewarding, *you can be sure you'll supplement this with negative contact.* Each of you has witnessed your child acting out in some way at the expense of being punished, grounded, reprimanded or physically spanked. Why? A TA group leader will show you how you collect bad feelings if you haven't allowed yourself to ask, give and receive good ones. Practice with other group members will reinforce your ability to love and accept love gestures, or positive strokes. You'll learn to reject negative strokes and avoid people who "walk over" you.

Some of us don't know how to arrange for pleasant contact, or we've forgotten how important other people are to our stroke survival. Marriage tends to make people rely on only *one* significant other for good feelings. Many men and women I know were surprised at the time of separation to find they literally cut off other relationships during their marriage. It takes time to build new friendships, but the investment is a good one. Which of you has remained sad and depressed in the midst of close, loving friends? If your sadness and grief is part of your normal grieving process, which of you didn't feel better having a loving arm around you, or a listening ear?

Take an honest look at *your* way of getting strokes in

the past. Did you get attention for your troubles, tears, or helplessness? Have you been feeling sorry for yourself? If so, you may want to change and discover you can be noticed, loved and stroked for existing—for simply being you! Each of us needs to be loved and recognized for BEING, not only for what we're doing. Many of us grow up with the idea that asking for strokes is impolite. Or, if we ask for a stroke then it's really not genuine. How many wives say, "If I have to ask my husband to take me out to dinner, I don't feel he cares about me." In other words, the husband, son, daughter "should" know what I need or want without my having to tell them. This is magical thinking and not realistic. As a child, your mother may have anticipated or intuited your needs accurately. Indeed, I'm aware how sensitive I am to my own children's wants, especially before they were old enough to talk. Once they acquired the power of speech, however, *I expected them to tell me.* I was convinced my own mother could actually read my mind since she knew exactly which hand had been in the donut jar. I decided as a young child I would never let my own children think I had magical powers. Some of this yearning to be understood without telling must be a result of our early close relationship with our parents. Tell people what you want, today, however, and don't rely on their being as sensitive to you as your mother was. How many men say, "I'm tired and want to go to bed," when they really want to make love. Check and see if you are sending clear messages.

Sometimes we are afraid to refuse strokes which are negative. As children we're taught to say thank you for the yellow ruffle dress even if we hate yellow and ruffles. If a male friend compliments you on the dinners you serve, you can accept his strokes for cooking and still insist you go out if cooking isn't your way of being stroked. Ask for the specific strokes that you want and refuse to accept plastic or unwanted ones.

Many males accept strokes from their women out of duty. When my husband comes home I may offer him dinner, an invitation to dine out, or tell him guests are coming. He may "act" pleased, yet *feel* better stroked if I left him alone to read a book. I don't know this unless he tells me. I dated several men who assumed I wanted to be taken to fine restaurants when I wanted to stay home curled up before the fireplace. It's my responsibility to tell people *how* I feel and *what* I want. Make it yours, too.

Claude Steiner, a teaching member of ITAA, wrote a delightful fairytale which has helped our family stay aware of our stroking patterns. Claude refers to positive strokes as "warm fuzzies" and negative ones as "cold pricklies." "Hey, Mom, you just gave me a cold prickly" is not an uncommon remark from my youngsters. Even our three-year-old understood the stroke concept through this story, for she quickly reported "Our dog is giving her puppies warm fuzzies by nursing them!"

Learn how to give positive strokes to those around you each day. If you tell your children they are irresponsible, lazy, sloppy, disrespectful and untrustworthy, you are giving negative strokes. By focusing on positive aspects of your children's behavior, you can help them grow without criticism. Since there is a direct correlation between positive stroking and reduction in negative behavior, it seems simple to stop stroking people for negative behavior. Identify what you DO like in others, and focus on that instead. Indeed, I've noticed that people who stroke others negatively, usually stroke themselves in the same way. The person who finds fault or blames another is usually just as hard on him/herself. *Unfortunately, we do most of our parenting out of a negative stroking position.* We tell our children what we don't like, or how they could improve, but seldom stroke them for what they accomplish. How many women are stroked for cooking, cleaning and caring for their children? It is *often our failure to perform that is noticed.* This is true for the male also. How many men get stroked for going to work and maintaining their families. When the support check fails to come, however, they are stroked by a summons into court.

When you change your stroking pattern, you may find that others are skeptical or think you want something in return. It may take awhile before those around you realize that your strokes are genuine and unconditional. I don't even like my children to thank me anymore since I feel they don't need to be grateful for my attention. Stroking and being stroked can be *free.*

Another way to increase your stroking economy is through Parents Without Partners, Inc.,* an international organization for single parents. It's the only national and international organization that studies the problems of the single parent and develops programs to meet their needs. Each local chapter may vary its programs according to the uniqueness of its membership; however, the goals and aims of PWP are concrete and specific. Membership in PWP is a stroke for healthy relationships, not only for you, but for your children. It was important for me after my divorce to meet others who were faced with the same problems, conflicts and indecisions as myself. It's an opportunity to discover you're not as different as you believed, and not alone either.

---

*At the time of this writing, Parents Without Partners, Inc., is considering a new name for its organization. Members have decided that a single parent is not really "without" a partner, or lacking someone. The new name may be Single Partners, Inc.

I personally felt protected as a member of a single parent organization. I'd not only forgotten how to function as a single in society, but was frightened at the thought of moving out socially. My scared Child needed and wanted protection from others. PWP can structure your time and direct your interests into new activities and relationships. At the same time, membership provides you with the protection needed at a time of crisis. You'll receive permission from other single parents to voice your fears and thoughts, and to deal constructively with your problems as a single parent. Permission to lead a normal sex life is an important permission for many newly divorced people. Permission to put yourself first, and to spend what little money you have on sitters, instead of toys for the children, is also important during the early stages of single parenthood. Too often, single parents put their children first and themselves last to compensate for the loss of a parent. Your children will not respect your martyrdom nor the feeling that you sacrificed yourself for them. Remember the Victim role and decide to be the Victor instead.

Once you have acquired protection and permission, you'll feel potent to handle your single state by yourself. Before long, you'll give yourself permission, as well as protect your own Child, as you continue to make new choices for you and your children.

Joining a chapter of the National Organization for Women (NOW) is another way for a single parent to meet, discuss and implement change. Discovering that my married sisters and brothers were also discriminated against, isolated and oppressed by unequal job opportunities and economic inequality gave me further courage to act and change my situation. Participating in a "singles group" in your area will further increase your supply of strokes and structure your time in fun ways. It's OK to have fun again; it's OK to enjoy being and doing exciting things with other singles.

Getting involved in work that you enjoy and feel good about is vitally important at this time in your life. If you're a working parent, it's important that your work fulfills your needs for positive strokes. If the job you had before you became a single parent was simply a "paycheck," look at other job possibilities. When family life fails to provide nurturing and positive recognition, a job which is stimulating and meaningful contributes to your supply of good feelings.

Before becoming a single parent, I felt teaching small children was worthwhile and rewarding. Afterwards I wanted adult companionship, contact, and a less demanding profession. A woman I know, who was perfectly content as a bookkeeper before her divorce, found herself isolated and frustrated on her job after her divorce. Getting into a "people profession" gave her the contact she wanted and needed. Another acquaintance of mine stopped working as a secretary and went back to school. For this woman, starting a new career at the age of thirty-five offered stimulation and adventure. Other people I've known in my groups use this period to reassess their values and goals and make changes to enrich their stroke economy.

Several men have taken time to develop hobbies and pursue evening courses leading to alternative job choices. Instead of sitting home lamenting their losses or the silence around them, they have gone out and structured their time in rewarding ways. Most males already have jobs, so fun activities involving others are more important to their survival needs. Men I know have enrolled in dance classes as well as courses to improve their body, weight and general physique. It's not only the women who care about their appearance after a divorce. Single parents tend to improve their appearance or at least take more interest in themselves. Some men have gotten hair transplants or had plastic surgery. If improving your appearance is part of loving yourself (Nurturing Parent), that's terrific. Your outward appearance, however, will not conceal unhealthy tapes. Be sure not to neglect interior renovation.

Local schools and junior colleges offer inexpensive courses specifically designed to reorient the single person. Your YMCA and YWCA also offer a variety of subjects to meet the needs of your entire family. Ask around and discover the untapped resources in your community. Consider ways of increasing your circle of loving intimates, and structure your time in a new and exciting way.

Before you became a single parent, chances are you structured your time to avoid intimacy. When people are in conflict they tend to avoid each other or play games, neither of which contributes to closeness. If you've been used to withdrawing into yourself through TV, sleeping, reading, work or alcohol in order to avoid your unhappy situation, don't do that now. Allow yourself to put aside meaningless activities or pastimes and develop sound, trusting and rewarding friendships. All of the suggestions above are designed for you to give up "Going Nowhere" behavior and develop "Getting On With" habits.

Your chances for getting out and getting on with living, learning and loving are limitless. Begin with a self evaluation. What skills, potentials or dreams did you have before you were married? Decide which ones you want to pursue now, or develop new interests to meet your present goals. There are hundreds of community service projects, or helping people projects you can indulge in; however, focus on *yourself first* before you extend help to others.

Begin by recognizing if you are in a "rescue bag" (looking for other people to "save"), determine what specific need you want to meet, or goal you've decided to work towards and choose accordingly. *Save yourself first.* If you join a PWP group to help others solve their problems and thereby avoid facing your own, you're in a rescue bag. Often members of A.A. groups structure time rescuing others instead of planning activities and developing relationships which are fun. Save yourself first. There will be time in the future for you to offer your services to others. Now is the time for you to feel OK about taking or being self-centered. Choose only those activities that will directly implement and help you get the strokes and contact you want.

Close your eyes and imagine that you're dead. Really feel that your life is over. You'll never walk this earth again. Ask yourself if you have any regrets. Ask yourself what you've accomplished. What are other people saying about you? Look at the people standing at your grave, and decide not only how you feel, but what you think about the answers. Write down what comes to your mind, and decide what changes you want to make NOW. How will you make them? Take a deep breath, relax and enjoy the fact that you're still alive and have time to change!

Look at Diagram 6 and determine where your relationships and activities are right now. If you find most of your life in the GOW (Getting On With) square, you're already a Winner. If "Getting Away From" or "Getting Rid Of" has been your pattern up till now, consider a better option to flight.

When Harold a fifty-eight-year-old client of mine came into therapy he had little left in his life. In the past month he had recently lost his job of thirty-five years and was in danger now of losing his wife. Although on heavy medication, he was in a deep depression. While examining his script, he discovered life for him was one long struggle. He "should" end up with nothing, just as his father had done before him. This is exactly where he was on entering therapy. Harold was raised by midwestern parents who never had fun. His father felt and lived life as a struggle and "never got out from under." Eventually, Harold's mother left him. Although Harold was an educated man, and had held a responsible job all his life, he managed to get himself fired to fulfill his childhood prediction. Since he had fully expected to work hard, struggle and not make it, Harold felt it was inevitable that he remain sad, unemployed and rejected by his wife. Harold needed permission to succeed without struggle. He also had to give up his "take care of everybody" script and begin taking care of his own needs. Again, Harold was following a program his father had designed. He was not living out his own thoughts and feelings. When Harold worked through these myths about himself, he made a decision to return to farming—his dream, and succeed in supporting himself and his family on the land without struggle.

Sometimes, "getting away from" can be a step in "getting on with" something better for you. It might, however, be your way of copping out. If you're a person who seems to "Get Nowhere" and finds that "No matter what I do, nothing works out," consider how you set yourself up to fail. Begin today by going where you want to go! Frequently, people in this square have not taken the time to find out what they want. They haven't felt important enough to put themselves first. YOU ARE IMPORTANT and you can change your position NOW by moving into a GOW position.

The "Getting Rid Of" square is OK at spring-cleaning time, but as a way of life leaves little to hold on to in the way of people or things. Again, there are always occasions for each of these behaviors. There are times when getting rid of a relationship is legitimate, and divorce necessary. There are times when a separation, or GAF is healthy. If you continue this pattern over and over, however, you may want to look at this boxed in position and opt for another one.

Cut out a big square and label it GOW—GETTING ON WITH. Paste it on your bedroom mirror so you and your children are reminded each day of your new decisions and goals. Our refrigerator is still used for this purpose since we spend more time in our kitchen than anywhere else! By now you can see that life is lived in different shapes. Triangles and Squares are not for you! Keep yourself and your kids whole by staying in a circle of winners!

DIAGRAM 6

FORMS OF OK

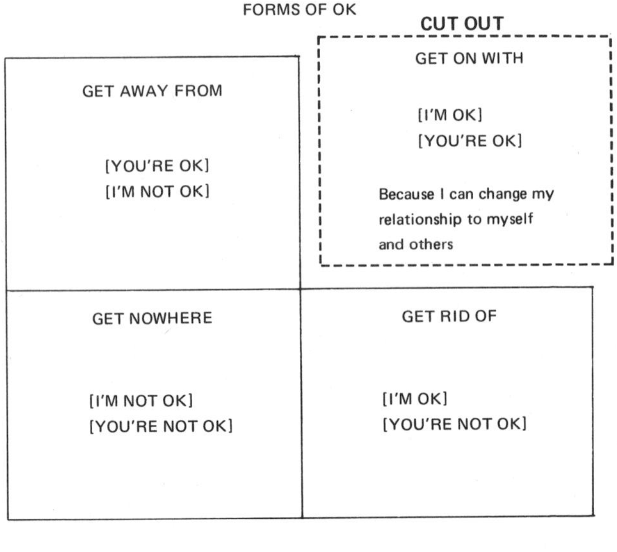

GET AWAY FROM [YOU'RE OK] [I'M NOT OK]	CUT OUT GET ON WITH [I'M OK] [YOU'RE OK] Because I can change my relationship to myself and others
GET NOWHERE [I'M NOT OK] [YOU'RE NOT OK]	GET RID OF [I'M OK] [YOU'RE NOT OK]

Chapter 8

UNHEALTHY GAMES

A "game " is a series of transactions between two people which results in bad feelings for both parties. We all learn to play games as children. If we're healthy, we continue to choose people who'll play games for fun. If as children, however, we learned to play games in a crooked way, chances are we're still continuing to do so. For example, our four-year-old daughter complained of being sick the other day and asked for special attention. Immediately her two-year-old sister said, "I'm sick too." The older child recognized at once what was going on and said, "Oh, Katie, that's a game. You just want Mom to hold you, too!" All the elements of a game were in that transaction. Katie was afraid to ask directly for special consideration. Instead, she decided to say she was sick. If she continues to get attention in this way now, later on she might continue to "play" sick to get recognition. Eventually, she'll really be sick.

There are a number of games particularly common to single parents. Each of these games provides a way of structuring time with another person. They also provide people with a way of contacting each other even though the contact is harmful. Sadly enough a game is usually not played in awareness so that simply telling a person, "you're playing a game" is not enough. If, however, you recognize that you have bad feelings after transacting business with another person, you can be fairly sure you've been "gamey." You can also count on your Child being the inventor of the game! When your Child wants something that your Parent or Adult won't permit, a game follows. Your Child will use any means to achieve its goals, and once you start a game, it's difficult to end before the payoff, or your bad feelings.

A typical game played by single parents is "Now I've Got You, You Son Of A Bitch." This game is encouraged by lawyers who attempt to get proof of misconduct on the other party. It is further carried on after legal proceedings end in an effort to "keep in touch" with the other parent. Phone calls to the absent parent pointing out failures, mistakes and irresponsible actions are ways of playing NIGYSOB. Here is a typical "Gotcha" conversation. This is considered third degree since the person is obviously going to continue playing harder and harder until she gets a good kick.

Mary: "Hello, George, I'm just calling to see if you paid the doctor's bills like you're *supposed* to according to the Decree. You know how *embarrassing* it is to go there and not have the bill paid."

George: "I'll take care of that tomorrow, Mary." (George gives definite answers to be sure Mary won't get him.)

Mary: "You're *supposed* to have the trust fund money in by September 12th and it's already the 18th. I could have my lawyer cite you into Court for that, you know!"

George: "According to my copy it said the 22nd, Mary," (George stays in his Adult, by giving information only and doesn't get hooked.)

Mary: "You know Andy is *really* upset with you. You don't give a damn about him. He cried his

poor little heart out when you didn't get him
Saturday."

George: "Mary, our son refused to go with me Saturday unless our daughters stayed home. I'm
not going to give in to his tantrums. He can be
part of this family and enjoy himself, or stay
home and be miserable."

Mary: "He stayed home all day from school and
vomitted. His grades are really bad now and
all he says is *"Daddy doesn't care about me
anymore."* He's *really* disturbed. I would
think your conscience would rot out when you
think of that *poor child*. (Now, Mary has
finally found the right place to "get" George.
She can get him by using the child as the
target.)

George: "Let me talk to him, Mary." (George is still
keeping his cool.)

Mary: "What's the use. . . You always did prefer
your older son more. Don't think Andy
doesn't know it. You took Paul on that camping trip and left him out. . ."

George: "That camping trip was for teenagers, I ex-
plained that to Andy. It's all that garbage
you've geen telling him about me that really
has the kid upset. *You're a no good bitch.*"
(Now, George has been gotten and Mary gets
her kick too. Both can end the game having
stroked each other negatively. Probably
before the divorce their main contact was
through negative strokes. Neither one wants
to stop the contact, yet neither one wants to
risk change and develop a new way to contact
each other.

Watching the absent parent for signs of misconduct, or questioning your children after returning from a visit, are direct ways of looking for something to pin on the other party. Citing a man into Court for failure to comply with some part of the divorce or separation decree can also be a way of continuing to "get" the other person. If your reasons for confronting the absent parent are Adult, and if you are merely giving Adult information, you're not playing a game. You won't have bad feelings and neither will the other person. If, however, you involve lawyers, friends, children and relatives in a battle of right and wrong—you're probably playing a game. It only takes ONE person to stop a game even though it takes two to play. If you've been collecting bad feelings in order to separate from a person, examine yourself and ask if it's still necessary to "prove" your decision was right! Ask yourself what it does for you to invest so much time and energy in negative feelings. Find out what you want to do with that time instead and avoid, ignore or refuse to play NIGYSOB any longer.

"Ain't It Awful" is another favorite game of single parents. Usually this game is played shortly after separation or death of a partner, but it can become a way of life. How many of you find yourself saying, "I just don't know how I can manage these children all alone," "I can't depend on that man to send a check on time." "It's just awful the way he's living with that other woman." "The way she dresses my kids, I'm sure she's spending MY money on herself." "Now that he's remarried, he pays more attention to his step-kids than his own." "I'm sure she's running around all the time leaving those kids hungry." "He promises to pick them up and keeps them waiting. It's just awful."

While these statements might be true, and in fact, probably describe the behavior of *some* single parents, your complaining about these situations will not result in change. Instead of using your vital energy to promote sad, angry and resentful feelings, act now to change what YOU can and ignore what you can't.

Remaining in contact with the other person is a way to keep yourself aware of his or her behavior. You don't have to call the other, and you don't have to visit after the divorce. Any form of contact is usually a game—a way of collecting information to feed your angry, sad or hurt Child. You can write a letter if you feel you do have something to communicate, or have your attorney write.

Many people continue to drive by the other's house, or attend parties, gatherings and activities where they know the partner will be in order to feel injured. Some women I know continue to ask for news about the other and feel bad once they hear the partner is, in fact, happy and content in a new relationship!

If you need help managing the children then ask for it in your Adult and not in your whiny Child. If a check doesn't come on time, have your lawyer handle that transaction. The personal, social and sexual life of the absent partner is no longer your concern. When a person makes it his/her concern, it is usually a game. Instead of admitting they are morally indignant or jealous, they insist the activity is harming their children. No child I know is injured at the thought of his/her parent having a loving other to care for them. My children, on the contrary, felt relieved to know their dad was well loved in his new situation. The fact he was not married did not bother them at all because it didn't bother me!

If she is spending YOUR money on herself—so what? The most nurturing statement my former ever made was, "Take care of yourself first because I know if you are well, the kids will be too." I have not ever met the mother or father who is irresponsible and negligent out of intention. What the departed sees or hears is usually a capsule of the situation anyhow. Your children report what *you* want to hear so be aware if you want to hear bad news, they will invent it for you!

If either partner fails to keep appointments with the children, then I would insist the child not be told until the time of the event. In this way, I prevent them from waiting or being disappointed. If he comes, it is all to the good. I could go on describing ways to solve typical problems, however, my vast experience has shown me that if a person *wants* to have problems—enjoys negative feelings and contact, he or she will *always* have something to feel upset about. So, primarily, it is up to you to decide if you are determined to remain in a combat situation after the divorce! If so, you will seldom run out of ammunition.

"If It Weren't For Him/Her" is another favorite game played by single parents. Before the separation, this game usually ended with one person being blamed for what the other person didn't have or wouldn't get for him/herself. Once separated, the pattern of making another responsible for failures, shortcomings or losses persists. "If it weren't for HIM I'd have a beautiful home, a nice wardrobe, good friends, happy children, or be able to work." "If it weren't for HER I'd have more money, a good sex life, peace of mind, a job promotion, freedom to be out with the guys and luxuries." If after the separation, both parties achieve their goals, perhaps the relationship did inhibit individual growth and achievement. If, however, you find you're still not capable of having a good sex life, lovely home, friends, fun with your children, chances are you've been playing a game.

I feel the roots of this game are so deeply ingrained in us as kids that we have to consciously ask ourselves *how we keep ourselves from getting what we want.* As a child we're truly dependent on the other. We do feel, "If it weren't for Mom and Dad we'd be_____(fill in your own blanks)." How many parents encourage this game by saying to a small child, "The glass of milk slipped," instead of "You dropped the milk." Or, "That nasty table hit you," instead of "You ran into the table." The other day I heard a father with three small kids swear and stomp his feet when he dropped a light bulb. "That damn bulb slipped and fell," he said. *It's difficult to assume responsibility and begin owning your own feelings and behavior again.* But you CAN do just that.

It's difficult to learn to take credit for mistakes as well as achievements and still feel OK. As a child grows, he learns to blame the teacher who is "mean, unclear and demanding"; he blames his brothers and sisters when things go wrong and eventually his parents for his failures and unhappiness. How many children say, "I'm bored" with the implied understanding that "If it weren't for you," they'd have some entertainment in the home!

All of these games are ways of saying "I'm not in charge. I'm unimportant. I'm not able to get what I want." Every time we play these games, we're taking away our own feelings of potency. We're admitting we're helpless to create and change our own lives. We're saying that other people control us.

"Wooden Leg" is another way of demonstrating your impotence. The purpose of this game is to prove you are not OK. A person who enjoys misery, and learned early in life how to be the "Victim" may still be looking for others to rescue or punish him/her. This can be a tragic game as children quickly develop "Wooden Legs" until a family is frozen in a state of woodenness. Parents encourage this game by saying, "John never did have the stamina to do things," or, "Mary always did have trouble remembering things," or "Phillip was sick as a baby and never did catch up," or "Helen, always did have stomach aches if you demanded things of her." The theme of this game in adulthood is: "How can you expect a woman with three small kids to. . ." or, "How can you expect children from broken homes to. . ." or, "How can you expect a man who works shifts. . ." or, "How can you expect a woman with no education and skill to. . ."

Ask yourself how long you've had your "Wooden Leg." How have you used it to keep yourself helpless? Discuss your fear of giving up your "Wooden Leg," for anyone who has never walked on his/her own legs will have a genuine fear of taking the first step. Ask yourself what you don't want to do, and be straight about it! You don't need a wooden leg to admit your real feelings, fears and wants clearly and concretely.

"Kick Me" is also a way of life for some people and can be a deadly game. We all know individuals who go out of their way to relate to people who abuse them. Eventually the kicked really believe there are only kickers in the world, and make sure they get their daily knocks. When Leanne came into therapy she was unaware of her Kick Me Game. She had just experienced a painful divorce from an alcoholic husband, however, and was determined not to make the same mistake again. During the marriage she had suffered internal pain as well as being the recipient of his anger and physical blows. All of her life, Lee had been used to taking abuse. In her own family she was frequently beaten and told she was not good, stupid and only worthwhile as a worker for the family. She supported her own family and after marriage continued to support her alcoholic husband. When their only child was seven, however, his abuse of her brought Lee to divorce. Since the divorce, she found all of her relationships with men were typically rescue ones. She wound up supporting, caring for and being responsible for men. Leanne trusted no one, and was hurt and withdrawn on entering treatment. She had little permission to be likable or liked.

Frequently, Lee would mention a "wall" which she felt she was "beating her head against." The "wall" was the same one her mother used all her life to stay married to an alcoholic. Lee recognized she was only willing to take a brick out of the wall in group. It was still difficult for her to reach out and touch others or allow others to reach out to her.

During a weekend therapy session, Lee struggled to dissolve the wall, and give up many assumptions she had about herself and others. She resolved to stay out of the Victim role and stop rescuing people. She expressed some of her painful feelings and felt safe enough to cry.

Lee's decision to say good-bye to her parents, who had little to offer her in the way of constructive advice or caring feelings, left her exhilarated and alive to make new friends who support her in her new life.

If you're accustomed to feeling put down or clobbered like Lee—ask yourself what YOU do to get kicked. If you find yourself saying "I've had it." Or, "I've taken enough of this," or "I'm up to here with. . .," you've been collecting kicks. You have a right to live and be loved without being humiliated, abused, used or neglected. No matter what your pattern has been in the past, you can change this pattern. Begin with an examination of your own self-worth, and end up refusing to be the target or grounds for others to dump on.

There are a number of other games which single parents play that are unique to the individual and to his/her particular script. A review of Eric Berne's *Games People Play*, will acquaint you with the ways these games perpetuate your bad feelings, interfere with healthy relationships, and eventually help you destroy your chances for being a winner. Remember, we're all born winners. We may have learned how to lose over the years, but this pattern can be reversed.

Chapter 9

CONTRACT FOR CHANGE

Once upon a time a little girl named Jane, and a little boy named Jim, discovered they could keep their parents happy and loving by doing what they were told. These children also found it was better to talk when told to, be pleasant and grateful, and in all ways follow the rules their parents set down. Sometimes these rules were unclear, and sometimes the rules were not even said out loud, but Jane and Jim were smart little kids and they knew what their parents wanted. So they changed. Each day they changed a little more so that eventually they forgot about their own hopes, thoughts and feelings.

As time went on Jane and Jim decided it was the same way at school. All they had to do was find out what the "big people" wanted, and there was peace, love and acceptance. Learning the rules was not as hard now because they had a lot of practice at knowing what OTHER people wanted. They could even figure out complicated messages so they seldom got into trouble. For example, when Jane's mother told her it was OK to wear her hair long, Jane knew her mother would feel a lot better if it was "short and trim." Jim was equally as bright, and knew that his dad really wanted him to be an engineer. It was OK to "fool around" with photography as a hobby, but no way to make a living.

Jane and Jim felt good because they knew they were BEING GOOD. They were following the rules. No one would get angry or leave them. They would be loved, protected and cared for so long as they lived by the rules. They believed this so completely that they were confused and frightened when someone did leave them. As a matter of fact, the older they got, the more puzzled they became as people disagreed with them or walked away. Something was wrong.

If Jane and Jim followed the rules, they SHOULD live happily ever after. They did follow the rules, and yet they knew they were NOT living happily, even NOW. NEITHER PERSON QUESTIONED THE RULES. Jim didn't think the rules were wrong, but instead felt "SOMETHING IS WRONG WITH ME." Jane also felt the rules were right, so she figured that "SOMETHING IS THE MATTER WITH OTHERS." Sometimes, when things got really bad, both of them decided, "SOMETHING IS THE MATTER WITH ME, AND SOMETHING IS THE MATTER WITH OTHERS, TOO."

It took a long, long, time until either Jane or Jim even thought that SOMETHING WAS THE MATTER WITH THE RULES. Once they questioned the rules, however, they were aware that the rules had to change and they did too. When they looked back over their lives, they saw that in the beginning they had changed to suit others. Now, they decided, they would change to suit themSELVES. It wasn't going to be easy, however, to find out who they really were. How were they going to figure out what rules they wanted for themselves? How could they discover what they REALLY felt about the rules they'd already made?

Jane remembered when she got angry as a little girl, she was sent to her room. Now she felt sad. Maybe she was REALLY angry, but had forgotten how to express that feeling. Jim remembered as a child when he was sad, he was told not to be a "cry baby." Maybe he wasn't REALLY angry now about that job he lost. Maybe he was sad instead, but afraid to cry.

Both Jane and Jim felt it wasn't easy to change. They knew sometimes it was hard work to discover what they really thought and felt. At times, they wanted to retreat and have life all ordered the way it was when they were small. Life was simple then and predictable. Sometimes they wished someone would still tell them what to do. It was hard to stop saying, "I don't know," and start figuring things out for themselves. It was even more difficult taking responsibility for what they did and said. All of their lives someone else had told them what rules to follow, so they really didn't have a lot of trust in their own power to direct their lives. At times the idea of taking charge of their own lives was frightening. Other times, they felt excited and even powerful to discover they could change.

During this entire process, Jane and Jim wished they could have help. One day, Jane met Jim and he told her about his wishing. The two of them started laughing because the Child in each of them knew that wishing on a star or a chicken bone didn't really work! Both of their kids still wanted to believe in magic, but their Adult knew better. Both of them knew that time and magic wouldn't solve their problems. Their Adult knew they had to do something NOW for themselves.

So, both these people joined a TA group and made a contract for change. They discovered in their group that they, too, were responsible for solving their problems. Jim found out he had to identify his problems and be willing to ACTIVELY change. No one was permitted to simply talk and do nothing. Jane found she couldn't make other people the cause of her problems. She learned that her children were not "making her feel bad," but that she was in charge of her own feelings. SHE MADE HERSELF FEEL BAD. That was hard. She remembered as a child her mother had told her to stop making noise because Jane had "made her feel bad."

Jane also remembered her father saying she "made him feel bad" when she refused to marry "that nice Polish boy" down the street. She guessed her parents really didn't know all the things she knew. They certainly never had any TA! Sometimes she even felt sorry they hadn't learned as much as she had. At those times, the therapist reminded her it was OK for her to change, even if they didn't.

Jim, however, was philosophical and decided his parents liked being the way they were. It was OK with him. Sometimes he told them how he was REALLY feeling and what he was thinking, and they listened. It wasn't important anymore that they agree with Jim's rules. He no longer needed their approval. Jane told her parents about her new discoveries, too, and they listened. After a while, Jane and Jim were surprised to find out that their parents had changed. Or, maybe, JANE AND JIM HAD CHANGED.

The most important difference, however, was in the way Jim and Jane felt. They really felt it was OK for other people not to change. The only people they really had to be concerned about was themselves. At first this sounded selfish. Secondly, this sounded like a lie since they had to live with other people. Most of their living in the past had been around rules and everybody had to follow them. Now, they could really see it was OK to be different. It was OK to change the rules. Jane didn't feel threatened when someone else acted, thought, or felt unlike she did. It didn't scare either one of them anymore to be different or to be who they really were. Both of them learned to trust their own feelings, thoughts, and experiences. Jane and Jim knew they were in charge now.

Jane and Jim looked forward to watching other people change in their group. Each week they could see and hear how other group members solved their difficulties. They learned more about themselves and their own ego states and found out that each of them had a lot going for them. It wasn't long before they realized that each person in their group was different, and yet they could love or respect each other's differentness. No one told them what to do, or how to do it. No one insisted they disclose their thoughts or their feelings. They were accepted for who they were, and Jane and Jim felt good about that. Sometimes they felt like they were in a family again, only this time the family was treating them like adults instead of little children. They were right because the leader of the group knew they had an Adult all the time and expected them to use it!

One evening when Jim and Jane were feeling really down in their group, they recognized their Child was in charge. Both of them felt safe, however, because nobody was going to hurt their Child in this group. Jim felt so safe he cried for many of the hurts he'd never allowed himself to feel before. He even remembered a pet dog that died when he was four and mourned the loss of his puppy as well as his other losses. Nobody told him to "Be a Man" because they knew his Child was crying. Everyone respected Jim's Child.

Jane finally got real angry one night and let herself shout and stomp her feet. She felt taller and more powerful standing up for herself. The other people admired her for saying what she really thought. It was good to hear Jane say, "I WON'T DO IT," instead of her sweet, placating voice saying, "I'LL TRY." Jim and Jane were experimenting with their thoughts and feelings. They were learning to be honest about what they felt. They were learning that some people accept honesty.

As the months went by, it was clear that Jim and Jane really didn't have to be in a group any longer. Both of them had the tools to deal with their own problems, feelings and thoughts. Jim and Jane knew that all their life they would have to make choices for themselves. Now they knew how to do this more effectively. It was time to say good-bye to their group.

Strangely enough, this is how the book began; another time for "letting go." The last evening in their group, Jim and Jane looked around at the people they loved and cared for, and felt like crying. They thought of the hours spent with these friends sharing their feelings and experiences. Neither one of them wanted to say good-bye.

Letting Go. Both of them realized all their lives they would be letting go in some way. Jim knew that even saying good-bye for a short time meant "letting go," and Jane knew that leaving her old job next month was another "letting go" process. Both of them had already "let go" of many out-dated and useless tapes. They had let go of many negative feelings and knew there was more space and energy now for good ones. It was OK to mourn the loss of the old, and it was healthy to feel excited about going on. Letting go wasn't so one-sided or lonely anymore. Jim and Jane were letting go in order to reach out to something new and challenging.

I hope all of you will take a look at what you've been holding on to, whether that means an unhealthy relationship, job, negative feelings or an unwarranted prejudice, and discover that KEEPING YOURSELF TOGETHER really means knowing HOW and WHEN to let go.

Chapter 10

THE SOUNDS OF PEOPLE CHANGING

As you read the following case histories, you may identify with the people, problems, feelings and experiences they have, but remember, people really are different. You are different and unique! It may help you to know that these people have similar life styles and problems, but still, you are a special person, an individual. The only real similarity between you and the people you hear and read about is that you, too, have experienced pain, anxiety, fear, anger, depression or some other self-defeating feeling. How you managed to collect those feelings, and the way in which you collect those feelings is different. It is important for you to identify your own script, however, and your own injunctions in order to lead a script-free life.

All of these people were committed to the process of change. All of them were equally afraid of change. Even though the pain of holding on was great, and in some cases, killing the person, still, as one man expressed, *"I know how to live with pain.* I'm afraid I won't know how to live without it."* So, another feeling that people have in common is that the unknown—even if the unknown will be better—is still scary. I am still scared at the thought of change.

None of these people took very long to change. Many of them were in treatment for a total of 36 hours. This doesn't mean they solved all their problems. It means they learned to identify, change and cope with the problems they had, and develop skills to help themselves.

They gave up destructive behavior and became their own therapists. The tools and behaviors they acquired will help them stay alive, healthy and sane. They learned and acquired a vast store of survival tapes and had completely retaped their destructive ones. They learned to recognize their own *authentic* feelings of despair, grief, anger, or sadness and felt that they had sufficient adult information to deal with these feelings now and enough survival tapes to support their Child in times of authentic stress.

When does a person decide to change? From my own experience and the feedback of others, I feel that when the pain of the situation is almost equal to the fear of change—the risk is taken. So long as a person feels they can survive within their script, they will. Often, however, a person has shut off his/her feelings, or tuned out his/her Child; they are not even aware of feeling pain. They may be on a self-destruct path long before any sign is noticed. In many cases, a physical symptom has to appear before the person is aware of stress.

Many males, for example, are permitted ulcers, backaches and chest pains. Women are permitted headaches, migraines and a number of female complaints. Most of us have permission to be sick. Many of us have no permission to admit we need help in solving problems! By the time our bodies have indicated our inner feelings or stress, we are out of touch with our lives, feelings and the circumstances we live with that cause stress. Going crazy, like getting sick, may be a device to circumvent the solution of psychological problems. When a person's Child can't find any other way to gain care, or when the need to be helpless and dependent is deeply programmed into the Child, the individual may seek a way to be admitted to an institution. At this point the Adult is blocked and the desire for change is usually dormant. The

Child may even accept the pain of shock treatments as a necessary punishment for being not OK.

Fortunately, permission to get help in solving problems is becoming more acceptable. I can see my dentist, or doctor, as well as my therapist, without feeling like I'm crazy, or ashamed and embarrassed to admit I need help. The people in these case studies all took a risk in deciding to look at their lives with a view toward change. They took responsibility for where they were, and discovered that in acknowledging they were responsible for their situation, they could also change. All of them had to give up the notion that *other* people or their circumstances were to blame for their unhappiness. Most of them had to "divorce" their own parents and let go of parental injunctions before they could begin to deal with their own feelings of divorce. They had to decide on the position of "I'm OK, You're OK" or the healthy position. Many came with the belief "I'm not OK and you're not either"—which is a futile position and could only end in depression and melancholy, suicide, crime, or institutionalism.

Those who came feeling "I'm not OK, but you're all right" had to regain their own feelings of importance. And those who felt they were OK, but others were the problem, sat alone with their feelings of righteousness and blamelessness until they recognized these feelings were hopelessly out of date in their present company.

Many wanted to make progress, and some did. Others realized that making progress was not enough to maintain an OK position with themselves and others. These people did not settle for "feeling a little bit better," nor did they accept "a little less depression or anger." Whether they would be "cured" or "make progress," as Berne noted, was clearly up to them. At no time, however, did any group member allow another to delude him or herself.

All of them said good-bye to many thoughts, feelings and situations. In saying good-bye, however, they discovered their hellos were more meaningful, genuine and right for them. They felt "more like themselves" and indeed they were, for living in script is living someone else's thoughts and feelings. Most of these people came in saying, "I don't like myself." When they regained their own feelings and thoughts, they left saying "I like what I see." "I like me."

CASE 1

Ellen, a twenty-six-year-old female, came into therapy following a divorce and a series of accidents designed to end her life "accidentally." In working within the group, Ellen discovered that since childhood she had been told she was "accident prone." Her mother, a reserved, controlled female, had seldom expressed feelings of concern for Ellen, and responded in an angry way to Ellen's hurts. Since this was the only attention she received, Ellen learned to hurt herself to get stroked. Ellen, herself, had no permission to feel anything but angry, and was not in touch with her own pain or hurt. When she allowed herself to accept the concern of the group, she discovered that all the broken bones, near drowning incidents, and car injuries were in fact scary and painful. A decision to knock herself off was revised when Ellen could see that even if she killed herself, her mother would not respond with anything but, "Well, I always knew she'd kill herself. She was *constantly* getting hurt as a child."

Paul, her seven-year-old son, had already begun having accidents, and Ellen could see how she was giving him the same messages. Like her mother, Ellen stayed busy and overworked, giving little time or attention to

Paul. The only time she stopped "rushing around" was when Paul got hurt. Then, like her mother, she paused long enough to inspect the injury, but acted annoyed and inconvenienced at the interruption. Ellen revised her decision that she was not OK and used her time to live constructively. Her new program for survival meant giving up speeding, avoiding highway signs, and in short, letting go of her mother who had lived out her life in pain and anger. Ellen took time to feel her own feelings and expressed them to Paul. She discovered that Paul responded to her caring just as she responded to the care of the group. Ellen has been accident free for two years and counts her birthdays from the day she gave up her suicidal script!

CASE 2

Larry, age forty-two, came into therapy after a series of conflicts with the law. Larry had a good job, but found himself "getting into trouble" all the time. He was an educated man, and held a responsible position which was threatened every time he did something illegal. There was no apparent reason for him to jeopardize his job, family or security by playing the game of "cops and robbers."* His wife had already asked for a separation, and refused to live with Larry's "games" any longer.

In looking back at Larry's childhood, he was aware that his mother had been proud of him when he did something dangerous. In fact, he could see that all his excitement came from doing dangerous things. He enjoyed "plotting and planning" so he wouldn't get caught! As a kid, when he got arrested, his mother appeared angry, but Larry was aware of her smile of pride. Her son was "clever and brave"! Larry's father was a timid man, and also felt proud of his son's ability to take risks with his life. It was only the intervention of a

---

*Berne, Games People Play.

high school teacher, whom Larry loved and respected, that kept Larry out of jail. This teacher had, in effect, given him permission to finish school, stay out of trouble and make it in business. As the years went by, however, Larry returned to his old games and injunctions. He had not really given up the unhealthy messages, or the need to find his excitement through danger.

Larry's therapy was difficult since he had never done anything for fun except get into trouble. He found life "boring and dull" when he was not "plotting" something. Even though separated, his wife was encouraged to join him in group so they could work together on constructive excitement! Larry's need to be in danger, in order to "feel alive," was replaced with lively activities which involved his family and friends.

CASE 3

Angie, age twenty-four, came into group as a result of one divorce and another marriage which was also threatening to end in divorce. Angie was an only child and was used to having her problems solved by her parents. For several weeks, she played "stupid," and insisted she didn't know what she was doing to cause problems in her marriage. Angie was sure "if it weren't for her husband," she would be happy. Looking into her past, Angie saw how she had run away from school and not graduated from college, run out of her first marriage, and even allowed her child to be raised by her parents. Angie had a long history of "not completing her assignments." She remembered that as far back as elementary school, her mother would fight her battles for her and complete her work.

Angie was scared to grow up. She was frightened now at the age of twenty-four to admit she was responsible. She was also tired of feeling a victim, so she contracted to stay in group and resolve her problems. Angie had a brilliant capacity for learning and solving problems when she allowed herself to make her own decisions. She decided that she was "tired of living on the edge of panic" and telling others they were "unfair" to her.

Her first "adult" decision was to remain married until she worked through her own injunctions. She took back the care of her own child and refused to run to in-laws or parents for protection or permission to grow up. During the course of her stay in group, she made a decision to finish college, and found she enjoyed using her Adult to deal with "messy situations" her script had created. Her husband entered threapy for a short time so he could understand how he reinforced her ideas and feelings about herself.

Hal was a bright, energetic man who liked to take all the responsibility. He further enjoyed her as a "helpless child" who stayed home and cared for him and all his needs during the first year of their marriage. He did not like her blaming him, however, or accusing him of stopping her from growing up. Hal also gave her permission to go back to school, and encouraged her to make her own decisions regarding the finances, home and maintenance of her own car. Gradually they formed a new relationship which allowed both of them to function as whole, autonomous people within the marriage.

Hal discovered he had his own "inner Child" and could laugh and play without needing Angie to program all their fun activities. He found he was able to feel strong and virile even though his wife contributed to the family finances, and was no longer threatened by her professional success.

Angie remained in group for nine months as she

continued to get reinforcement for "doing her own thing" and succeeding! As this couple became free of their scripting, the parents of both felt left out and lonely. Hal and Angie dealt with these relationships, and learned how to develop ways of staying in contact with their parents, without being tempted to slip back into the old dependency roles. Both Angie and Hal have remained out of therapy for three years and have had one child in that time. Angie's older daughter and new child are independent. Their mother does not complete their assignments for them!!!

CASE 4

Charles is a minister who came into group at the age of thirty-five as a result of his divorce. Charles was unable to admit to any problems which led to the breakup of his fifteen-year-old marriage. During an early session, he found himself saying "I'm perfect as far as I know, or nearly so."

In order to maintain this position, Charles had to stay out of touch with his feelings of pain, scare and isolation. He kept himself busy in church, and was known for his happy, cheerful disposition. Inside, however, Charles was scared. Charles was raised by a father who, "had his guts kicked out, but wouldn't show it." His mother was a sick woman who had been taken care of and protected from any problems. When Charles was little, he learned not to tell his mother anything but good things. All of his other feelings were blocked in an effort to protect her.

Charles could see that as a minister he collected everyone's feelings and didn't show his own. He was "saving" them, too. The effect, however, on his own life and personal relationships was devastating. At the age of thirty-five he had no close friends and his wife had deserted him. His voice was dead and controlled when he spoke of his own situation, yet he determined to get to feeling within the group.

Charles was in group for over a year before he exposed himself without fear of someone dying or being hurt. His relationship to women was healthy as he discovered that most females were unlike his mother and would not fall apart. He is currently dating a woman whom he will marry, and both feel confident he can remain with good feelings and still admit to mistakes. He gave up his "Jesus" script and opted for his own script-free life before he became a dead martyr!

CASE 5

Francis Marie, age seventeen, was referred by the school counselor as a withdrawn, uncooperative girl who was having difficulty at home and school. She was an attractive girl who felt "ugly, awkward and fat." Actually, she was slender, pretty and graceful! In the course of a marathon workshop where Francis Marie stayed for three days she worked through the original impression she made about herself as a child. Stories and conversation about her birth were remembered as she painfully recounted and experienced them in the group. Her mother and dad had both wanted a son. When Francis Marie was born, her mother told her that she was not only disappointed, but refused to take her home from the hospital. She insisted the doctor had made a mistake. Francis Marie was *not* her child. "Where's my son" her mother shouted. This story along with her name (which was Francis for the son her mother wanted) helped her decide she was unlovable as she was, a girl. Francis began gaining weight and in many ways made herself unlovable and ugly. When Francis was six, her father divorced her mother, which further confirmed her feelings that she was unlovable. Everytime she visited her father in his own home, and saw him playing with his young daughter, she felt rejected. "If he loved me, he would have stayed," she insisted.

When Francis entered high school, she began taking care of her physical appearance and emerged as a beautiful woman. She did not, however, acknowledge this change, and still saw herself as "an ugly duckling." Not only did she redecide this issue, and resolve her feelings of guilt and isolation, but she began calling herself by her middle name since Francis was never her anyhow!

The new Marie stayed in group for four months working on letting go of old behavior that had reinforced her "be unlovable, alone and ugly" script. She spoke loud enough for others to hear, and came to group dressed in becoming and feminine clothes. At the end of group, she had several friends of both sexes and felt comfortable for the first time with guys her age. Marie had an unusual ability to forgive her parents and the mistakes they made, and even initiated much on her own part toward being close to them. Her mother responded with enthusiasm, and seemed content with the new Marie even though she did not understand the name change, or the origins of Marie's problems.

CASE 6

Robert, age twenty-one, came into therapy as a result of a suicide attempt during his junior year at college. Bob felt oppressed and isolated when he entered the program, and was sure his problems were "in his genes." He said his father, grandfather and great grandfather had all "messed up their lives" and failed in spite of their intelligence. Bob had no zest or enthusiasm for living, loving or relating to others. His dad was a "loner" and had divorced his mother when Bob was twelve. He had been raised by his mother, who was a hypochondriac, and offered Bob few positive messages for staying alive and being well. He felt that he was a burden to her and his father. Both parents had made him painfully aware that "if it weren't for him," they wouldn't have married. His mother still held *him* responsible for the fact she had been pregnant out of wedlock.

Bob felt he was not only an unwanted child, but that he'd never had permission to be born to live. As he grew older, his feelings of rejection caused him to reject others. His college career was brilliant, but devoid of any fun or enthusiasm. He was toying with the idea of eventually freaking out on drugs altogether and had fantasies of driving his car off a cliff!

Since Bob didn't permit himself to express his scared feelings, he was unwilling to do so in group. He seemed determined to prove we were like his parents, "no ears and deaf." Further, his need to "grow up and take care of himself" left Bob with little sense of his "inner child" or capacity for fun. He was stuck with computing and only giving information in the group. During the third session, Bob became attached to another group member, Allen. Through Allen, he was able to explore and trust his own feelings. When this happened, he was willing to work within the group, and let go of his anger, scare and resentment toward his parents. Instead of killing himself with these feelings, he expressed them openly to people who heard and acknowledged him. "Nobody ever listens to me" proved to be untrue. Bob's decision to stop perpetuating these messages left him open to healthy relationships at home and eventually back at school.

Bob graduated from college and has found many nurturing parents along the way. He has allowed himself to get close to women who are not sick, and discovered females are fun and nurturing, too. The decision to live was, however, the first breakthrough in a script that offered him only failure, isolation and despair.

CASE 7

Helen entered therapy after a nervous breakdown. Helen had remained unmarried after her divorce, and was forty-two at the time she entered group. All of her life she had remained attached to her father who told her "I'll always take care of my little girl." Even after she physically grew up, Helen felt like a little girl and needed to be taken care of by everyone. She went from job to job until she finally ended up working as a secretary in a state hospital. Her mother approved of the job, and though Helen didn't like it, she remained there for fifteen years. One of her mother's greatest fears was that Helen would "go crazy"—a fear she had about herself. Helen's job at the hospital kept both of them safe since she was already in an institution!

Helen, had over the years, loved many men, but managed to find some way to end the relationship and feel depressed and lonely again. She was aware she was not "being taken care of by her father at all." He had, in fact, failed to support her even as a child. As an adult, she chose men who would prove helpless to love her, thus perpetuating her "Don't trust men" script.

A decision to stay sane was an important one for Helen. She stayed in her Adult and enjoyed her inner Child as spontaneous and not "crazy." She began enjoying relationships with others too. Helen had not worked through her fear of men, but decided to leave group content with living alone and liking it for the rest of her life.

CASE 8

Jeffrey, a thirty-two-year-old divorced male came into group with a sexual problem. Jeff had been unable to sustain any relationship with women during his adult life. He had many fears involving closeness and his own sexuality. In group, Jeff discovered he had always relied on his mother who gave him heavy messages to take care of her. In caring for her, he had even become a physician. As he climbed the success ladder, however, he was aware of a deep "emptiness" within himself. This "hole" was an avoidance of females.

Jeff's dad had been a successful dentist, but had not been close to his wife. Jeff had never seen an adult male relate to an adult female other than to care for each other's physical comfort and needs. He was aware that his father spent much time withdrawing from his family into science fiction books and television. There was almost no interaction or playing at home. Jeff himself knew he created situations to avoid intimacy. Much of his free time was spent alone in his room studying or doing research work, much like his father.

Although Jeff had his own apartment, he still had not made a decision to grow up. Emotionally he held on to his childhood and even acted the role of "little boy" on the job. He realized his colleagues did not accord him the respect he had earned, but treated him as a "boy."

Permission to say good-bye to his mother's destructive messages gave Jeff the ability to pursue females as an adult male. Further, he contracted to get involved in many activities which involved other people in a fun situation. Instead of satisfying his own sexual needs, Jeff established a relationship with a nurse at the hospital who related to him as an adult female and not a "rescuing mother."

Jeff accomplished much in the year he remained in group, and still calls from time to time to report how he has changed his life. He is still unmarried. However, he has enjoyed dating and is functioning on the staff of a hospital as a senior physician!

CASE 9

Sally, age twenty-six, came into therapy at the end of a long, unhappy affair following a divorce. Sally had been living with Matt for four years with the hope he would "eventually" marry her. The four years had been full of depression and anxiety for Sally until the breakup. Now, she was filled with anger and resentment for what she considered "four lost years of swallowing shit."

The message Sally identified before entering therapy indicated she was a bright girl with a good deal of self-awareness. Still, she had been so busy "taking care of others" most of her life she believed she would never accomplish anything for herself." Sally's feelings of self-disgust were so intense, she found herself repeating a slogan in her head from childhood: "everybody hates me, nobody loves me."

The first step for Sally was to find some way she would feel respect and integrity for herself. Nothing she was currently doing contributed to her feelings of self-worth. The job she had, the car and house in which she lived, were all subsidized by her lover. Much of the time Sally felt extreme anxiety at the thought of being financially unable to take care of herself. She contracted to get her own job, return to college in the evenings and finish a course in education which she had begun four years ago. She further decided to end the relationship with her former lover though she admitted this was "one piece of shit" she wanted to hold onto for a while longer. Members in the group encouraged her to call them for support during this period rather than Matt who used her feelings of insecurity to further his own need for power and control with females.

Sally's therapy took over eighteen months as she learned to take care of herself, stay out of "victim" roles and control her own situation. Her feelings of anger disappeared and the nagging depression which had been with her most of her life dissipated. She got in touch with her own feelings of excitement and self-worth as she realized her ability to change.

CASE 10

Carl and Elaine, a married couple of twenty years came into therapy when Elaine announced she was getting a divorce one day without any preamble.

Carl said he felt "sad and abandoned" by Elaine and didn't understand why she was suddenly leaving him. He said he was unaware of any difficulty in their marriage and appeared genuinely confused by Elaine's firm decision to leave.

Elaine appeared confident although angry that she had waited twenty years to take this step. She felt there was no way to repair the relationship, and simply "wanted support" for her decision to "make it without Carl."

During the course of the three hour interview it was apparent that since Carl worked six days a week and was frequently away nights and weekends, he and Elaine had seldom operated as a couple in the marriage. Each had led his own life, independent of the other except where "major household decisions" were needed. The care of the children was left to Elaine since Carl was absent much of the time. "The children have no respect for me, anyhow," he complained.

Elaine felt with their children grown and away at

college her function as a mother was greatly reduced. In addition, she no longer needed to maintain their large home. Carl was able to afford a housekeeper and maintenance man. She realized they had no financial problems and that her working was not needed, but "necessary for my survival." Carl felt scared and lost at her decision to work outside the home. Even though he seldom stayed home, he felt it was necessary for her to be there "all the time."

Carl refused to negotiate with Elaine so that they could remain married. He was unwilling to accept her working and also unwilling for her to develop friends apart from his business associates. She, on the other hand, was no longer willing to entertain his friends and attend business functions. Each one refused to cooperate in any way to change their life styles.

Elaine said she had "saved up all those twenty years" and deserved to do exactly what she wanted now. Carl, felt injured and unappreciated since he had "given her everything a woman desires." Her pleas for help, companionship, closeness and warmth, however, were not heard. Nor, was she hearing his crying abandoned Child! Both tuned each other out a long time ago, and were simply "killing time."

Elaine entered therapy as she wanted to learn and change within a group structure. Carl was unwilling to enter group as he saw the divorce as final and irrevocable. He felt once the proceedings were over, he would easily find a woman who would appreciate the fine home, position in the community and freedom to spend money he was able to give.

CASE 11

Rosie, age fifty-two, came into therapy when a second marriage was on the "brink of disaster."

Rosie had married at the age of sixteen to get out of a "sticky home" situation. Her parents had never gotten along and according to Rosie, there was never enough to eat, much less enough clothes to go around. Rosie recalled going to bed at night early so her mother could wash her only dress and dry it before school in the morning. She was aware that the man she chose was really a young boy who had no dreams and ambitions, but anything was better, or so it seemed to Rosie, than staying home.

Her marriage to Ed lasted long enough for Rosie to have three children, and from the time she was twenty-four until forty-five she lived alone with them, working as a telephone operator to support the family. When Rosie met Phil, she thought her days of loneliness were over. She even fantasized quitting work and simply being a "housewife and mother."

A year after the marriage, Rosie regretted her decision. Phil lost his job and Rosie found herself supporting him as well as caring for the home, meals and maintenance. Feeling "cheated" as she had when a child, Rosie was determined to find out what "was wrong with her." Why couldn't she have what other people had? What was she doing wrong?

Rosie had no permission to stay married. Her own parents had found marriage a "cross to bear" and a struggle. Her mother had lived out her senior years in loneliness and poverty. Rosie wanted more for herself. She was unable to stay married to Phil, however, as he was unwilling to take any responsibility for the relationship. She did realize that her old script messages chose him for exactly that purpose. When Rosie left group, she felt she had made several new friends who contributed to her well-being. She felt important, and knew she had stopped "cheating" herself by avoiding men who needed rescuing.

People who change sound different. Their voices change. In the beginning, a voice may be whiny, plaintive, dull, and droning; or strident, loud, and full of anger. Some voices are so small we have to ask, "What did you say?" Some voices are boring, monotonous, and dead. Other voices are mumbled; words are swallowed so no one knows what is said. Some are fast and staccato: anyone listening wants to cover their ears or shut out the sound. Later, voices are melodic; they have a wide range of tone and tempo. The person is *alive* and wants other people to listen and respond with aliveness to him or her.

People who change use different words. Instead of using phrases like, "I'm falling apart," "I'm running around like a chicken with my head cut off," "I'm over my head," or "I'm drowning in a bottomless pit," they choose other phrases to describe their feelings. "I'm flying high," "I feel like a bubble, full and floating," "I feel like a Christmas child opening boxes and boxes of goodies—and those goodies are all in ME." "I'm full of the excitement of being alive."

People in the process of change give up passive language. Where they once said, "If only I knew how I got myself into these messes I might be able to avoid them," they later say, "I'm not going to get into battles anymore. I'm a retired general!" They give up phrases like, "I can't help feeling panicky," "I don't know how to express myself," "I'm unable to say no." As these people change, they discover their own power, and the power is reflected in their new language.

"This decision is for *me*. It's not to please anyone else or to make anyone else happy." "I can fit in my own pieces to my puzzle. *I can do it.* I'm not a helpless child anymore."

"I've stopped thinking *about* doing and *I am* doing."
"Hell, I'm not panicky I'm really *excited* about taking that risk."

Instead of rehearsing what they are going to say, people are spontaneous. They give up editing before they speak and burst forth with their own authentic thoughts and feelings. In the place of lies and myths they discover their own truths about themselves and the world they live in. Sometimes the lies that people live with are really big. Here is what they sound like:

"If I change, my husband will run off and leave me."
"You have to be married, *but* you have to be unhappily married."
"My husband is scared of my success, so I can't succeed."
"If I'm too strong, a man won't love me."
"Nobody will love me if they find out what I'm *really* like."
"I don't remember important things. That's the way I am. I have shit for brains."
"I'm too dumb to know what I want."
"There is something in my brain that limits me."
"I should feel hurt and pain when I make a mistake—then I'll learn my lesson."
"I've gotta work before I play and there is *always* work to do."
"I don't deserve to live. My mother died giving birth to me."

Eventually these lies are uncovered and become laughable. In a short time people come to truly *feel* the lie is exactly that—an unwarranted assumption. When they discover or redecide important issues they can say, "I do deserve to live. I was *not* responsible for my mother's death." "I *am* lovely and beautiful and intelligent. *Look at me.* I really *am.* " "I don't have to kill myself working—or drive myself into a heart attack. I am playing and enjoying, and that's OK. I'm OK." "I actually *enjoy* making mistakes now. It shows I'm human. I *can* be married and I *am* married and happily!"

People who change don't ask permission to talk. They don't say, "Could I please tell you this," or, "Is it OK if I ask a question?" They simply speak. On the other hand, they don't have to talk all the time either. They can be silent and feel comfortable in that silence. They can interrupt if it's important, or choose not to interrupt. Essentially, they have *freedom of choice.* They are not predictable any longer. They are not static, nor do they respond to situations in the same way. They are open to change, to risk and to continued growth. They are closer to the selves they were at birth—trusting, excited, curious, and spontaneous in their feelings—they reach out to others instead of withdrawing with fear.

Many of these people call after they say goodbye. They call to simply keep in touch—to say hello again and share what they have made happen for themselves. Sometimes I don't recognize their voices. Their changing goes on. Often I laugh when they report how people close to them have changed. I suspect that those "others" have not changed nearly as much as they think. Now, however, they don't need them to be changed in order to live or work harmoniously with them. They discovered that unlike the time when they were children, others really don't have to make their worlds safe and secure for them. Each of us can function autonomously and without fearing to live in his own skin. I am certainly happier and more complete when those special "others" do care about me. I admit I feel better, too, when someone I love stands in the same place that I do, but if they are not there, I can still survive.

In the beginning our own well-being did depend on a few others. Our very lives were dependent on them. We excluded others or were excluded simply because of our age. This exclusion was related to sharing good feelings too. We loved the members of our family. We kissed, hugged, and cuddled with a limited few. Out of this early exclusion an erroneous belief emerged: "Not many other people *really* give a damn about what happens to me. I can only be close and open with a few people." As adults we continue to limit our relationships without finding out if others care. We don't really tell or show our feelings to others. This limiting process serves a purpose. If I keep others walled off or distant from me, I won't experience the hurt of rejection. Sometimes I don't even know that I do this. I really believe that no one cares or that only my parents, mate, or close friends care. Slowly each of us discovers that many people are invested in other human beings—if they are allowed to be invested. How important I feel when others invest themselves in me by sharing with me their hopes, dreams, joys, and disappointments. Sometimes, it's true, there might be no one around to do so. Or the someone who is around is not interested in what I am feeling or thinking. Yet to assume that any form of reaching out will yield the pain of disinterest is to accept being alone.

Most people don't want to be alone. They learn again within the new "family group" how to reach out and trust. At first when one person is absent they may feel abandoned all over again. "Where is *everybody,*" a young man asks when really it's only Ellen who is missing. He experiences anger and rejection when he has exciting news and someone important to him is absent. "If Sue cared about me, she would be here tonight," is one reaction. People learn how to look at this old feeling of hurt and to evaluate it anew. They discover that Sue's absence doesn't have to diminish their pleasure or pride in accomplishment.

What about those who don't change? What do they sound like? Many people ask that question. "Surely, *everyone* who comes to you doesn't make it, do they?" No. Every person who experiences pain or dissatisfaction with himself or his surroundings does not change. Many choose to remain with their old beliefs, feelings, and nightmares. What about them? How come? I don't know. I have some assumptions which I have shared with you throughout this book. However, I, too, am still looking for the answer to that question. I'm sure there are as many answers as there are people. I've not written here about those who have chosen to remain with their failings, fears, or depressions. I do know that the number of those who do so are few compared to those who accept the challenge of change. I am further convinced that everyone is capable of changing their life and that while they may not do so *now*, it's possible that they will, in the future.

I have a close friend who is a dentist. One day I thought about what Tom does in his office all day and what I do in mine. It occurred to me that there were similarities. Many people take care of their teeth before they have serious trouble. Others wait until the abscess or the pain of a toothache drives them to the dentist. They can't ignore their mouth any longer. After the dentist fixes the tooth they may have their entire mouth X-rayed and repaired, or they may go home and forget about the rest of their teeth until the next pain. I'm not suggesting that if a person has good dental hygiene he will also have good mental hygiene, but there are similarities. It takes time to repair teeth. It takes money, too. And it's not always painless. If I have the permission to spend money, time, and concern on me, then I'll do it. If I trust the dentist and feel he will consider my fear and be sensitive to my pain, there is even more incentive to make that appointment.

And, so people who have changed care about themselves. They care about others, too, in a more genuine way. They care enough about themselves to help themselves, and enough about others to allow them to do the same.

People who change sound different. When you put this book down walk around and listen to the people where you live. How do they sound?

APPENDIX

APPENDIX

TRANSLATING INTERNAL COMMUNICATION

The design of the pathways of communication is as important as the design of walkways in a city. If the critical routes in a city were not designed to facilitate the flow of traffic there would be chaos. Or, as in Berlin, where a wall prevented any flow of traffic there was a complete breakdown in traffic and communication. When transportation designs are constructed to facilitate the flow of traffic everyone moves smoothly. We still have to stop sometimes, and there are warning lights; but we know that the "go" light will come on, too. Berne identified such critical routes in the human mind when he perceived that the Parent could say "stop" or "watch out" and that the Adult could say "go" along with the Child.

Anyone who violates a traffic law gets into trouble. When one of us disobeys an injunction, we, too, may feel we're in trouble. We may *feel* that we are going to be fined or punished. And because those rules were probably all Parent rules, it's most likely that blocks are between the Parent and Child.

©1973 Boyce Productions
Terra Linda Sta. Box 6278, San Rafael, Ca. 94903
Set V: New Concepts; No. 18: New Ways of Viewing Personality

Historically, at least, most of our internal discussions took place between our Parent and Child. We had very little Adult, and so even now when we have Adult information, many of us still continue to hear the "Don'ts and Can'ts" and block the flow of communication our Adult has at its disposal.

This *internal dialogue* can be much different from the one going on outside ourselves. Many people aren't even aware they have an internal dialogue until you ask them, "What did you tell yourself in your head about that?" Obviously, we aren't aware that internally we have shut off or blocked one ego state. We don't identify that we have silenced an important part of ourselves.

When a client of mine discovered that his only conversation was between his Critical Parent and Scared Child he was floored. No wonder he felt such despair. From the time this man got his feet on the floor in the morning, his Parent was threatening him. Frequently, he believed the information was Adult. "He was in fact stupid. His I.Q. was inferior to those around him, and he didn't have the mental stamina of most of his colleagues." This hurting, internal flow of messages was thoroughly cutting off—or blocking, any possible flow of nurturing.

In Transactional Analysis we analyze those transactions which we *hear* going on between people. We see that each exchange comes from the Parent, Adult or Child ego state in one person and is received or answered by an ego state in the other. This outward communication, however, is usually a result of the internal communication. They seldom sound alike. Often people will say, "I heard what you *said*, but what did you *mean*?" Instinctively we are aware that much of what we mean is *internally* felt and not verbalized.

Arthur Rissman, a consultant in personal problems,

also finds as much importance in the *internal flow* of feelings and ideas as he does in the external transactions. This "internal dialogue" has its own design and "critical routes" and language. Using the PAC model, he visually created a way of analyzing the process within the mind. It looks like this: The small pac with the ego states shows that we have developed historically a complex PAC. We absorbed, in each of our ego states, messages that "got through" and became a part of ourselves from the outside world—i.e., we "learned" in one way or another. Much of this process is discussed elsewhere among TA theorists, as well as among thinkers from other systems. Here, we are primarily concerned with the general procedure.

When the flow moves smoothly, we function well; when the flow is blocked or broken, we have problems. Thus the primary, historic blockage may be between the Parent and Child. For example, the Parent wants the Child to remain a child and never leave or grow up. The Child wants to get married, move away and take care of herself. The Parent can only give hurting or prejudicial messages to the Child on this subject. Thus, the hurting blockage exists. The flow of messages from the Adult to the Child is interrupted, or the information that the Adult gives the Child is unrealistic. For example, the Child may respond rebelliously and say, "I can take care of myself." (Even though neither person has a job.) Or, "We love each other so much that we'll work everything out." (Implying that "love" is enough.) Or, the Child may comply and feel sad and hurt. "OK, you're right. I'm not able to make it without you, Parent."

In either case, the Child is a victim. Whether the Child reacts rebelliously or compliantly matters very little. The decision is not based on Adult information, with parental approval. The Child loses and so does the Parent. The latter loses because the intention of the Parent is to help the Child grow up, and the Parent has failed to do so.

How do we resolve these internal communications? Since it is not possible to get rid of destructive or prejudicial beliefs, the expert in communications looks to collaboration with them. I look to see which ego state has the most power. If the Child is internally rebelling and saying "no" to everything, or complying and saying "What can I do next to please you," then I want to talk to that Child with my Nurturing Parent. If the Parent is overwhelming and critical-threatening and abusive, then I still want to talk to that Critical Parent with my Nurturing Parent. Once I have managed to get the ear of the Child and the Critical Parent or Controlling Parent (and both listen well to nurturing), we can work together to look at Adult information or options.

Returning to Rissman, he has developed a color design for clients so they can further understand what is going on internally. Rissman colors his ego states to suggest the nature of the internal dialogue: Yellow is for C—vibrant, positive, energetic; Blue is for A—intellectual, cool, peaceful; Red is for P—sensing danger, active, carrying the blood line. As the ego states collaborate, they become P-C, Orange, a lively flow or clash; C-A, Green, growing, strong; P-A, Purple, royal, super parent.

Most of the people in these case studies colored themselves Green for growing even though they began early in life to turn on the Red sign for danger—and limited themselves. Most, if not all, began as children to fit into the triangle which kept them from living in a colorful, alive world. Each one felt a victim, rescuer or persecutor. All of them had experienced divorce, or were children of divorce. This does not mean that divorce in itself develops these roles, since many parents who stay married also perpetuate the triangle. I suspect, however, that in families where divorce had occurred, children have more permission to split, and lack permission to be close. Further, when as children, we are unable to see adults solve problems together, we assume this can't be done. Thus, many people come to therapy feeling they must "do it themselves." Or, that two people simply cannot live harmoniously together—there is always the theme of one parent being powerful and one weak. Cooperative and enjoyable parenthood seems to be a rare exception.

The tragedy, however, is that none of these people got out of the triangle by leaving their original families. Most of these people entered marriage believing "my marriage will be different." All of them had hopes and dreams that they would "not make the mistakes my parents made." Somehow, they knew better. Actually, *all they knew was what in fact they had known and experienced as children.* Until they became aware of new learnings, they had little choice or hope for change.

These are people who have experienced pain. They recognized their own feelings and wanted to do something about their situation. They were people of hope. Not all of them had permission to get help. Often a wife gave permission to a husband, or a husband gave permission to a wife, to spend the time and money on therapy. Sometimes, the children gave permission.

These people were honest. They committed themselves to an experience of growth and accomplishment and achieved much for their short time in group. They discovered that many people receive unhealthy messages, or translate messages from people around them in unhealthy ways. Each felt comfort in knowing "they were not the only ones" that felt a certain way.

Each week these people published their findings on

their sheets of paper for all to see. These "advertisements" are hung up so that each member, as well as the person, can see their growth and change. In the beginning the blank piece of paper has their name and position on the top—within a few minutes in group much more is added! Slowly, as people work their problems, group members hear injunctions, and when this happens, the person has the choice of working through an old injunction and decision or holding on to it a while longer. These sheets of paper, however, record the person's own words, feelings and decisions. They record contracts for change and re-decisions. It is not unusual for group members to recall what is on these sheets without even looking up!

A typical sheet looks like this one:

Peggy Blake   Aug 12

1. Position: I'm OK, you're not

2. Injunction: Don't Succeed,
   Don't Grow Up, "Don't
   Do Anything."

3. Feeling: Angry, "lonely,
   separated, no place
   to go, rigid, frozen in
   one spot." "I'm
   like a mummy - dead-
   rigor mortis has set
   in."

4. Games: Yes, "But" and "If It Weren't For You."

5. Remarks: "Every attempt to do anything independently met with gross disapproval."

6. Decision as a child: "I'm going to get out of here, or stay frozen."

7. Contrast: "Unfreeze so I will move."

8. Lie or Myth: "If I unfreeze and do what I want, I'll die or go crazy."

Redecision: "I moved and I didn't die. I made my own choices and I didn't get killed for them!"

Each week as the group assembles there is much activity as people walk up and cross off old injunctions—or old business that they dealt with on their own during the week. In some instances, the beginning of group resembles the old time revival meetings where people announced their "sins" only here they announce their achievements! There are as many strokes and attention given to those who come feeling OK as those who come feeling not OK. Each member, however, becomes a trained clinician in listening for unhealthy tapes.

Some of the messages these people continued to send to themselves were crippling in a number of ways. For example, with many, their health was impaired, and for others their relationships with intimates. Many were unable to grow on their jobs, and felt economically unsuccessful and frustrated. While we receive thousands of messages growing up, it appears that there are only a few that can destroy large areas of our capacity to live lovingly and winningly. Many of these messages are woven throughout the samples.

As you read over these case histories again, you will find people who were unwanted from birth, or denied the ability as children to truly be themselves. You will discover on close inspection that many were not permitted to express their feelings, or feel comfortable being close to the opposite sex. Others, were not given messages for success and remained stuck with unwanted jobs and relationships. *The purpose of the family is to supply human beings with survival tapes.* Where those tapes are weak, lost or inadequate, *we must reach for other ways to parent ourselves.* Within the group structure, we are able to give each other messages which replace or displace old, unhealthy ones, and develop ourselves so that each of us feels our own personhood.

A beautiful woman, who celebrated her first birthday within our group, summed up this whole chapter by saying "Good morning to you, good morning to you, I gave birth to *my self* and so can you!"

GLOSSARY

GLOSSARY

ADULT: An ego state that is not related to a person's age. *Everyone* has an Adult. This is the objective, computer part of the person which weighs and decides reality without the interference of emotions.

AUTONOMY: Parental approval, informed adult, and child spontaneity.

CHILD: This ego state contains all the *feelings and impulses* that come naturally to a child. The Adapted Child experiences and feels the way he was taught, and the Natural Child expresses him/herself freely, spontaneously and autonomously.

CONTRACT: An agreement between a person and the therapist, or person and group which states a particular and specific goal or change desired by the person.

CONTAMINATION: When the Adult takes in and believes as true unwarranted Parental beliefs or Child distortions. The boundary of the Adult is contaminated.

DECISION: A childhood commitment made as the result of an injunction to be, feel and act in a certain way regardless of the consequences. (Most destructive decisions are out of the person's awareness).

INJUNCTION: A prohibition or directive which a Parent gives to a Child (usually not verbally), which the Child may act on out of awareness.

INTIMACY: Game-free behavior without the desire to exploit or the fear of being exploited. The Child is the originator of intimacy.

LIFE PLAN: What will happen to you as a result of your script.

LOSER: Someone who does not accomplish what he/she sets out to do.

NONWINNER: Someone who breaks even.

PARENT: An ego state adopted from parental figure in the past. It may be nurturing and caring, or critical, prejudicial and controlling.

PERMISSION: The ability a person has to disobey or ignore a parental injunction if it is destructive.

POTENCY: The power of the person, group or therapist to deal with the injunction and the feeling experiences as a result of an early destructive decision.

PROTECTION: Support and information from the person, group, or therapist needed to reinforce and protect the Child in the process of change.

SCRIPT: A life plan based on decisions made in childhood and reinforced through either negative or positive stroking.

STROKES: A unit of recognition, either verbal, non-verbal or physical which is positive or negative. Strokes are necessary to survival so that even negative ones become necessary if no positive ones are in the environment.

TRANSACTIONAL ANALYSIS: A theory of human behavior which is based on transactions occurring between three ego states, Parent, Adult and Child.

DECONTAMINATION: Becoming aware of the misinformation in order to deconfuse the Child and strengthen the Adult is the first step in decontamination.

DRAMA TRIANGLE: A diagram showing the possible switches that take place in a game or script. The three major parts are Persecutor, Victim and Rescuer.

EGO STATE: A consistent pattern of feeling and experience directly related to a corresponding consistent pattern of behavior. Unlike Freud's ego states in that anyone can observe, hear and identify ego states. They are not unconscious entities, but knowable and recognizable.

GAME: A series of transactions between people (verbal or non-verbal) designed to structure time, get strokes and support a person's position. A game is out of awareness and always has a pay-off in bad feelings.

SUGGESTED READING

Berne, Eric............................*Games People Play*
New York: Grove Press 1967

Berne, Eric ....*What Do You Say After You Say Hello?*
New York: Grove Press

Harris, Thomas A. ....*I'm Ok—You're Ok*
New York: Harper & Row 1967

Birnbaum, Jack ....*Cry Anger*
Don Mills, Ontario: General Publishing Co. 1973

Edited by Bohannan, Paul..................*Divorce and After*
Garden City, New York: Doubleday 1971

Leonard Campos & Paul McCormick......*Introduce Yourself To
Transactional Analysis;* Berkeley, Calif.: Transactional Pubs 1969

Callahan, Sidney Cornelia ....*The Working Mother*
New York: Warner 1972

Ernst, Ken ....*Games Students Play*
Millbrae, Calif.: Celestial Arts 1972

Ellis, Albert ....*How to Prevent Your Child from
Becoming a Neurotic Adult*   New York: Crown 1966

Freed, Alvyn M. .............................*T.A. for Tots*
Sacramento, Calif.: Jalmar Press 1973

Hirsch, Barbara B. ....*Divorce: What a Woman Needs To Know*
Chicago, Ill.: Henry Regnery Co. 1973

Jongeward & James...........................*Born To Win*
Lafayette, Calif.: Addison-Wesley Publishing Co. 1971

James, Muriel ....*Born To Love*
Lafayette, Calif.: Addison-Wesley Publishing Co. 1973

Kubler-Ross, Elisabeth ....*On Death And Dying*
New York: MacMillan 1969

Satir, Virginia...............................*Peoplemaking*
Palo Alto: Science & Behavior Books Inc. 1972

The Journal of PWP, Inc...................*The Single Parent*

Tazewell, Barbara Raymond Brown..........*Would You Believe
I Was Once A Happy Princess?*   Akron, Ohio: B/W TAI

CELESTIAL ARTS BOOK LIST

LOVE IS AN ATTITUDE. The world-famous book of poetry and photographs by Walter Rinder. 128 pages, clothbound. $6.95; paperbound, $3.95.

THIS TIME CALLED LIFE. Poetry and photography by Walter Rinder. 160 pages, clothbound, $6.95; paperbound, $3.95.

SPECTRUM OF LOVE. Walter Rinder's remarkable love poem with magnificently enhancing drawings by David Mitchell. 64 pages, clothbound, $5.95; paperbound, $2.95

FOLLOW YOUR HEART. A new and powerful companion to the fabulously successful Spectrum of Love with illustrations by Richard Davis. 64 pages, clothbound, $5.95. paperbound, $2.95.

THE HUMANNESS OF YOU. Walt Rinder philosophy and art rendered in his own words and photographs. 64 pages, paperbound, $2.95.

GROWING TOGETHER. George and Donni Betts' poetry with photographs by Robert Scales. 128 pages, paperbound, $3.95.

VISIONS OF YOU. Poems by George Betts, with photographs by Robert Scales. 128 pages, paperbound, $3.95.

MY GIFT TO YOU. New poems by George Betts, with photographs by Robert Scales. 128 pages, paperbound, $3.95.

YOU & I. Leonard Nimoy, the distinguished actor, blends his poetry and photography into a beautiful love story. 128 pages, clothbound, $6.95; paperbound, $3.95.

SPEAK THEN OF LOVE. Deep and sensitive poems from Andrew Oerke with beautifully illustrated drawings from ancient Asian texts. 80 pages, paperbound, $3.95.

WILD BIRDS AND OTHERS. Poetry rich in imagry and depth of compassion from Wendy Long. Beautiful photographs by Ron Sugiyama. 80 pages, paperbound, $2.95

WHERE DO YOU GO FROM HERE? Poignant, funny, always moving, one-liners in a circus of photographs by Robert Weston. 64 pages, paperbound, $2.95.

I AM. Concepts of awareness in poetic form by Michael Grinder. Illustrated in color by Chantal. 64 pages, paperbound, $2.95.

SONG TO THEE, DIVINE ANDROGYNE (Seven Steps to Heaven). A Psalm of Praise for the new age integrating modern psychology with ancient religion by Rowena Pattee. 128 pages, paperbound, $3.95.

GAMES STUDENTS PLAY (And what to do about them.) A study of Transactional Analysis in Schools, by Kenneth Ernst. 128 pages, clothbound, $6.95; paperbound, $3.95.

A GUIDE FOR SINGLE PARENTS (Transactional Analysis for People in Crisis.) T.A. for single parents by Kathern Hallett. 128 pages, clothbound, $6.95; paperbound, $3.95.

THE PASSIONATE MIND (A Manual for Living Creatively with One's Self.) Guidance and understanding from Joel Kramer. 128 pages, paperbound, $3.95.

DREAMS: Messages From My Self. A sensitive effort aimed at helping individuals appreciate and interpret their own dreams by Ruth Kramer. 80 pages, paperbound, $2.95.

THE SENSIBLE BOOK (A Celebration of Your Five Senses.) Barbara Polland awakens the understanding of their senses for children. 64 pages, paperbound, $3.95.

THE LIBERATED MOTHER GOOSE. A bold stroke in behalf of the re-education of children and their parents from Tamar Hoffs. 128 pages, paperbound, $3.95.

THE SPORTS TIME MACHINE. Newslike text and pictures of the great moments in the history of sports by Dave Brase and Tim Simons. 96 pages, paperbound, $2.95.